9-28-70

The Challenge of Economics

THE CHALLENGE OF ECONOMICS

A Guide for the Perplexed

ALBERT ALEXANDER

Pitman Publishing Corporation

NEW YORK LONDON TORONTO TEL AVIV

Library of Congress Catalog Card Number: 69–16863
Manufactured in the United States of America
Designed by Tere LoPrete
1.987654321

For Roslyn

Contents

PART THREE INTERNATIONAL PROBLEMS

PART FOUR EPILOGUE

Preface

The challenge of economics is basically a challenge to every person in America to understand the underlying forces that make up our economic system and the economic systems of other nations.

Economics is generally understood to be that subject mainly concerned with the study of the way goods and services are produced, distributed, and consumed. It is the social science that analyzes man's attempt to utilize his resources to provide for society's wants. It deals with the way he makes his living.

We have endeavored here briefly to illustrate the theory and practice of how one system—the market economy—attempts to provide goods and services that people need or desire. By way of contrast, we have included an analysis of how others attempt to solve the challenge of economics: determining what a society shall produce, how it will be produced, and for whom it shall be produced. Above all, to use President John F. Kennedy's words, we have attempted to describe "the practical management of a modern economy."

ALBERT ALEXANDER

List of Figures

PART ONE

BACKGROUND and STRUCTURE

CHAPTER 1

INTRODUCTION

Making Economic Decisions

The challenge involved in making economic decisions is not restricted only to specialists, or factory managers, or bank or government officials, or even to economists. It is a challenge to everyone who must face a lifetime of choices. Essentially, these choices involve resolving rationally the basic conflict between our wants and the scarcity of resources to implement or obtain these wants. All resources—land, labor, managerial ability, chemicals, metals—are limited, or scarce, in quantity. But the demand for these resources, as well as the products produced by applying and combining them, is insatiable. No society—no matter how rich in resources—can satisfy all the wants of all its people.

THE MEANING OF SCARCITY

It might be wise at this point to consider the meaning of scarcity. No doubt many readers will raise their eyebrows at the very thought of scarcity, living as they do in a land of abundantly stocked supermarkets and department stores. But it is easy to be misled by common usage which frequently differs from the specialized terminology of a discipline. In this book, we shall discover that economics, too, has a language of its own.

In the parlance of the economist, scarcity does not necessarily mean that goods are rare or difficult to obtain, nor does it imply dearth or famine, as one commonly uses the term. (Goods refer to items that satisfy human wants.) *Scarcity*, as the economist defines it, refers to goods that are not free. This, in turn, introduces the subject of *free* goods, items like air, water, and sunshine that are abundantly provided by nature and are available without cost. But even these goods would be considered scarce if we had to pay for them. Good drinking water, for instance, is difficult to obtain in many parts of the world. When sold in containers, it loses its status as a free good and becomes a scarce or economic good.

Economic scarcity exists even in highly industrialized nations such as ours because man finds it easy to raise his standard of living, to demand more goods and services as readily as they become more available. If variety is the spice of life, scarcity is a basic fact of life. For variety demands that goods and services be provided from the resources of a limited nature. No society has ever been able to supply all the products people need or want, in the particular form and amount desired, at the specific place and time they are wanted. Economic goods are, of course, additionally scarce because our means of obtaining them—mainly by money—are limited in relation to our wants for them. Thus scarcity is a *relative* matter rather than an absolute condition.

Some societies and some persons are more affected by scarcity than others. By any economic standard the United States is wealthy. But as any child knows, many of the goods and services of this rich economy are not readily available to all people. As any informed citizen realizes, not all the worthy programs considered by the federal government can be undertaken at any one time. A war, for instance, may cause the nation to postpone attention to urgent domestic problems. However, compared with developing nations, our scarcity problem seems negligible, especially in view of our high standard of living and tremendous output.

Even a brief look into a farmer's home in India quickly reveals the difference in the meaning of scarcity. Peering into the windowless mud hut we observe a single piece of furniture—a straw mat that serves as a bed. Wood or brass bowls and plates, and some pottery jars comprise the cooking utensils. Running water, electricity, and a sewage system are conspicuously absent.

India's per capita income is slightly more than $50 a year, which about equals the weekly per capita income in the United States. In rural areas, where more than 80 percent of India's population lives, per capita income is $35 a year. More than 160 million people earn less than 20 cents a day! To be liable for income tax, an Indian must earn the equivalent of $44 a month, and in the population of 510 million, fewer than 3 million are that well off. Given these low incomes, and a tremendous population scrambling for the limited agricultural and industrial output, India's scarcity problem is an obvious one.

If we relate the concept of scarcity to the problem of making economic decisions, scarcity becomes more understandable from an American point of view. Should the family purchase a new automobile, or should they buy a summer home? Should savings be used toward a child's college education, or should they be used for renovating the house? This list of alternatives is numerous. Our inventive society prides itself on its frequent "new and improved" additions to already available possibilities. In view of this abundance, wants have a way of multiplying, but incomes to attain these wants remain relatively limited. Thus, choices must be made from among the many alternative ways of spending limited income.

Similarly, leaders in business and industry constantly face economic choices and must devise a system of preferences (or priorities) for producing the most desired goods and services. Priorities must be determined for what is to be produced and how it will be produced. If management decides to produce color television sets, it cannot with the same resources manufacture electronic equipment for space capsules.

Economic societies, then, must ascertain how to allocate their limited resources. Naturally, countries rich in resources, like rich people everywhere, find it easier to satisfy more of their wants than do poor countries. Somewhere in their list of wants, however, both wealthy countries and well-off people find it necessary to draw the line. Thus, in the United States, we ask: Should we invest our resources into putting a man on Mars, or should we invest in the education of our young? Should we budget for a $40-billion anti-ballistic missile system, or should we improve the conditions of our poor?

Additional goods and services can be produced without choosing between alternatives only if there are sufficient *unused* resources. This means that raw materials must be available, as well as necessary manpower and properly tooled factories. (Again, remember that if resources *are* being used for one purpose, they cannot be used at the same time for another purpose.) In any event, the real problem for any economic society, confronted by alternative choices, is to get the most out of its limited supply of resources by producing those goods and services it thinks are most wanted. In so doing, the most efficient methods must be used to produce these goods. A system *economizes* when it derives the greatest output of goods and services from its supply of labor, raw materials, and such man made resources as tools, machinery, and factories.

Thus far we have concentrated on the positive choice to be made. Economists insist, however, that the way you choose *not* to spend your money is also a factor. These turned-down choices are referred to as *opportunity costs.* The opportunity cost of using your $5 for a football game is a record you did not buy, or two movies you did not see.

The opportunity cost to a businessman of producing radios is represented by the television sets he chose not to make.

THE NEED TO ALLOCATE RESOURCES

Choice is fundamental to economic decision-making. An individual producer, and eventually the entire nation, must decide how to allocate or put to best use the available resources. These productive resources are relatively limited and thus need skillful economizing and management. Economists generally describe resources under four headings: *natural resources, capital, labor,* and *management* (entrepreneurship.)

Natural Resources

Natural resources include land and its uses, such as for growing food, for sites, for erecting factories, and for minerals such as coal, iron ore, and petroleum. The air and the sea, too, supply natural resources (for example, oil from the sea and nitrogen from the air).

Capital

Capital consists of man-made resources such as tools, machinery, equipment, and the factories that are used to produce other goods. (Capital also consists of money needed to purchase equipment.) In a steel mill, both a hammer and a continuous strip mill 80 feet or more in length are capital, for both contribute to furthering production, by substituting mechanical energy for the more arduous human effort. We are all familiar with a bulldozer, which turns one worker into an army of workers, and with a computer, which transforms a single operator into a battery of electronic clerks. Thanks to such spectacular, yet routine, equipment, American manpower is remarkably productive. It is estimated that in the United States today more than $20,000 worth of equipment is behind each industrial worker. It would be difficult to overemphasize the importance of capital to production.

Labor

In economics human efforts fall into two basic categories: labor and management. Labor involves man's ability to perform the many tasks calling for the production of goods and services. Jobs range in degree of difficulty from unskilled porters and janitors to highly skilled atomic physicists and space engineers. The value of a worker's productivity depends upon his ability, education, and technical know-how, of course.

Management

Management represents a specialized skill that continually aims at better ways of seeking, finding, and organizing the necessary natural resources, capital, and manpower to develop productive enterprises. Managers on this level of economic activity are generally referred to as entrepreneurs.

Entrepreneurs continually face the problem of economizing, that is, how best to use the productive resources—the natural resources, capital, and labor—that are needed to produce goods and services. If they choose to use their land for an office building, they cannot (at least economically) use the same land for a factory. If equipment is created to manufacture automobiles, the same equipment cannot be used to manufacture typewriters. Human resources are endlessly varied, but the same human beings cannot be engaged in producing perfumes and airplanes at the same time. In other words, the cost of using resources to satisfy one collection of wants is that the resources cannot at the same time be used to satisfy another collection of wants.

THE BIG QUESTIONS OF ECONOMICS

Multiply these problems and you have the problem of an economic society: how to decide to use limited resources to satisfy human wants. All societies, from the most primitive to the most complex, must find answers to these fundamental questions:

1. What commodities shall be produced and in what quantities?
2. How shall commodities be produced?
3. How will the output be distributed?

What Commodities Shall Be Produced and in What Quantities?

This leading question in turn encourages other questions. What is the nation's stock of resources, their costs and prices? What is the standard of living—the tastes and actual purchasing power—of the people? What is the technical ability of the nation's workers? Do they have the knowledge and skill to produce supersonic planes, for example, or must the economy be content with simple commodities because knowledge and skills are lacking?

Another obvious question concerns the matter of priorities: Which goods come first? Before consumer goods such as washing machines, television sets, or refrigerators can be produced, producers' goods (capital) must be available. Only by investing (spending) in capital goods can any society ever hope to have consumer goods. The Soviet economy has continually invested in capital goods at the expense of consumer goods in order to build an industrial society, a war machine, and a space industry. In our economy, wartime tilts the balance in favor of defense products over consumer items.

How Shall Commodities Be Produced?

In attempting to answer this question, the producer is guided mainly by the need to combine his resources in so efficient a manner that his costs of production will be kept as low as possible. This, of course, is a matter of choice. The entrepreneur must decide on the types of labor and materials he will use, the specific equipment he needs, and the methods that will permit production at the lowest cost.

For example, a road can be built of asphalt, gravel, or concrete. In countries such as China and India it is possible to use many laborers and few machines because of the abundance of human labor. In the United States, it is more practical and cheaper to use more machines, and even complicated ones, to shorten the many arduous and expensive man-hours. Thus bulldozers, earth-movers, dump trucks, spreaders, and cement mixers are more frequently seen on the landscapes of advanced economies where labor is relatively scarce, and therefore more expensive. In examining how commodities shall be produced we soon discover that there are many ways of producing each product: One resource may be substituted for another in the process of attempting to produce efficiently at the lowest possible cost. Will synthetics or natural fibers be used? Aluminum or steel? Plastics or metals? Cost obviously will be a vital factor in the decision. Above all, technology involves the application of new scientific approaches to machinery, chemistry, and power to produce new products or new techniques in making products. And, again, the techniques used will be those that will reduce the costs of production.

How Will the Output Be Distributed?

Societies vary in their ways of dividing the goods and services they produce. Some seek to establish a method of dividing the products more or less equally, at least in theory. (None, however, has succeeded in bringing about equality of income.) Other societies quite frankly recognize various degrees of inequality of distribution. Thus there are societies where traditions maintain a pattern of rich and poor. Such societies are more frequently to be found in communities where agriculture is the prevailing way of life. A few hereditary families own most of the wealth, while the mass of the population inherits a much less enviable status. Many societies, including the United States, tend to reward the individual on the basis of the importance of his particular contribution to the value of the finished product. Under this system, the messenger boy in an atomic energy plant obviously will receive considerably less income than the plant's engineers or chemists. As we shall discuss in greater detail later, this type of society also insures individuals certain minimum standards of living, regardless of their productive contributions.

All societies organize social systems in order to choose what to produce, how to produce, and for whom to produce. Societies fall into two general categories: the centrally planned economy, or command-directed, society and the market-directed, or free enterprise, society.

Simply stated, a command economy is directed by a small planning group, which makes the big economic decisions for the country and supervises their execution. Such economies are invariably accompanied by a political dictatorship. Leading examples of command economies are the Soviet Union, Communist China, and the Communist nations of Eastern Europe.

HOW A MARKET SYSTEM ANSWERS THE BIG QUESTIONS

A market system, such as the one that operates in the United States, decides the basic economic questions through the response of producers and consumers to prices set in markets. This is a price-directed system, which relies on the profit motive and on competition to produce wanted goods and services. Government also has an important role in the market system, as we shall later see, as a sort of overseer by enforcing rules for fair competition and by taking various actions to keep the economy healthy.

In a market economy, private citizens may enter into and conduct businesses in the hope that they will make a profit by producing or selling what they expect consumers will buy. Goods are produced for exchange—for labor, natural resources, or capital—expressed in terms of money prices. The actions of countless buyers and sellers are guided by these prices in countless markets. Ultimately, consumer demands backed by dollars send the signals to producers to supply the wanted goods and services in the quantities desired.

Changes in prices serve to regulate the market economy in basic ways. We have mentioned the great variety of methods of making individual products, and how resources may be substituted for one another in production. Price determines how the producer will use his scarce materials. A carpet manufacturer, for example, may switch to nylon or to an acrylic fiber if wool is so expensive that it would drive the price of producing carpets up. By choosing one of the lower-priced man-made fibers, the manufacturer is permitting the higher-priced wool to be used where it may be in greater demand, such as in the clothing industry. This stronger demand reveals that consumers are more willing to pay a high price for woolen clothing than they are for other items made of wool. Thus consumers help to determine the allocation (specific uses) of resources by discouraging their use if they are scarce and their prices are high, and encouraging their use when they are plentiful and prices are low. Essentially, then, the marketplace, where supply and demand operate, determines the priorities of the limited resources among the more numerous wants.

Producers respond to price changes by producing what is profitable and avoiding what is not. When consumers are interested in an item, they are willing to pay higher prices, thus making it more profitable to produce. Decreased interest means decreased prices, which can result in decreased profits and lead to decreased production.

Consumers, as we have indicated, are profoundly affected by prices. How they will spend their money depends mainly upon prices—keeping in mind, of course, their particular tastes and incomes. Consumer preferences and prices in combination determine what the output should be. Since producers similarly affect, and are affected by, prices, they jointly (with consumers) decide the uses for our productive services and the goods and services that will be produced.

How do people get the income that enables them to "vote" or to participate in the economy? Households sell to businesses their labor for wages and salaries, their land (or other resources) for rent or lump sums, or their money for interest. Businesses sell their products and services to other businesses and to households.

Revenues from sales are used to cover the costs of production. Profits, it is hoped, will also be present to keep the business afloat.

THE "FLOW" OF INCOME

Note below the "flow" of income among the various factors of production: the workers, creditors, landlords, and businessmen. Cost and income are opposite sides of the economic coin. Consumer purchases (expenses) give income to the businessman. Labor costs to the businessman represent income to the worker. Like the coming and going of the tides, income flows through the economy. Producers' costs, in the hands of the consumer, become spending income. In turn, this income is spent for the producers' goods and services. Spending creates demand for production; business firms, in return for profits, attempt to satisfy these demands.

Prices, as we have indicated, act as a cement to keep the market system together. Competition among businessmen serves a similar purpose. If only one businessman controlled each product on the market, the market system would not work, or it would work very badly. This lone manufacturer, if he made television sets, for ex-

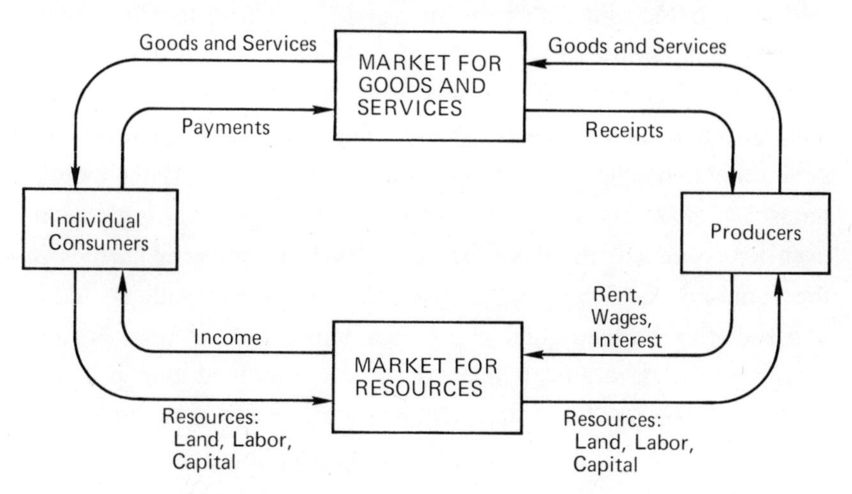

Fig. 1. The flow of money, goods, and services in the United States economy.

ample, would have very little incentive for improving his sets and for reducing his production costs. Competition, however, tends to force producers to charge the lowest price consistent with their ability to make a profit and stay in business. If one manufacturer charged a higher price for his sets, competitors would find it profitable to undercut his price.

Since, however, there is more than one manufacturer of television sets, each manufacturer attempts to use the resources necessary for production in his industry as efficiently as possible. The prices that the average television manufacturer pays for goods and services are almost the same as his competitors pay. He must, therefore, keep trying to be more efficient. He must keep these costs down in order to meet his competitors' prices. Examining the situation of his labor, capital, and natural resources, he must evaluate the most efficient use of labor, the present quality of his machinery, and possible need for new equipment. He also must interest himself in research and development to keep abreast of improved technology in his industry. Research may favor him with a new or improved product. It may also improve his production techniques, so that his aim of keeping costs down and profits up can be realized, or provide him with substitutes, such as transistors for tubes, that may cut his cost.

Prices and competition are worthy regulators of the market system, but they need added support. This support is provided by government, which helps to enforce competition, regulates certain industries, and attempts to keep the economy growing and on an even keel. Indeed, the government today is so active a partner in the economy, especially when we consider its tremendous taxing and spending budgets, that many economists use the term "mixed economy" to describe changes that have modified our price-directed, free enterprise system. Many of these changes, which we shall discuss in Chapter 3, are due to the increasingly greater role that the federal government is playing in our economy.

GOALS OF AN ECONOMIC SOCIETY

Finally, it must be kept in mind that an economic system is also guided by certain social goals that help determine the direction in which a nation wants its economy to grow. Thus any solution to an economic problem will be influenced by one or more of the following social goals: economic growth, stability, personal security, freedom, and justice.

Economic Growth

Economic growth involves providing for increasing production for the future to satisfy the growing populations that will demand more and better goods and services. Through economic growth we help to insure higher standards of living for this and other generations. Improvements in technology represent one of the major avenues for progressively increasing the total output of goods and services over a period of time.

Stability

Stability exists when an economy is continuously fully employed. This goal aims at keeping the economy balanced, avoiding both the depths of depression and recession with their unemployment and "bad times" and the heights of inflation with its accompanying unsettling and unjust situations. Insuring stability means that we try to avoid the "ups" and "downs" and strive to keep the economy on a healthy course.

Personal Security

Personal security attempts to provide income for individuals by reducing economic dependency incurred by unemployment, sickness, and old age. Citizens desire steady employment, and if a crisis occurs they expect to be provided for by various forms of Social Security.

Freedom

Freedom gives the consumer liberty to choose the goods and services he wants; it gives the producer the right to open or close a lawful business; and it guarantees the worker the right to choose his own job.

Justice

Justice consists of fair treatment for all persons and all groups in the economy. It proclaims equal opportunity regardless of race, creed, color, or sex. Together with freedom, it constitutes an important segment of an economic bill of rights.

For various reasons, these social goals are not fully attainable, nor can they be attained all at the same time, for at any given time some goals may be in conflict with others. For instance, if we want full employment of all our resources, then there is a danger of inflation; hence the goal of economic growth runs into conflict with that of stability. Freedom to make business decisions may be curtailed by decisions to set wage and price controls in the interests of stability. Freedom to travel may be restricted in order to help the balance of payments—a goal of stability. Personal security for workers, such as union guarantees or Social Security benefits, may run counter to the freedom of the employer. These are some of the more obvious contradictions in society's pursuit of social goals. The list of these contradictions of course can be extended and multiplied.

Priorities must be arranged according to the order of desired fulfillment, and in cases of conflict society must determine which goals are more important. It must decide the goals which should be given attention before others—and how much attention each should receive. Above all, it must be recognized that social goals must be decided by political votes, just as the consumer influences the economy with his dollar votes. Although this book concentrates on the economic aspects of our free enterprise system, it should be obvious that no economic system stands apart from its political, cultural, and moral atmosphere.

Essentially, the challenge of economizing is that individuals and societies must participate in the task of best utilizing scarce resources for the efficient production of wanted goods and services. Men organize economic systems in order to allocate these scarce productive resources and to distribute incomes that will permit the purchase of these goods and services. Individual decisions set the pattern for the free enterprise or market-directed system of the United States. Prices, responding to countless decisions, exercise a major influence on the workings of the market-directed system. Government interferences in the market are strong enough to cause the system to be labeled a "mixed" economy. No economy, it should be added, including our own, operates in a vacuum. Society insists that the economy be guided toward certain goals for the common good: economic growth, stability, security, freedom, and justice.

President John F. Kennedy in 1962 graphically described the challenge of economizing: "What is at stake in our economic decisions today is not some grand warfare of rival ideologies which will sweep the country with passion but the practical management of a modern economy. What we need is not labels and clichés but more basic discussion of the sophisticated and technical questions involved in keeping a great economic machinery moving ahead."

CHAPTER 2

PRODUCTION

Improving Living Standards

The challenge to improve living standards for a growing population can be stated very simply: We must produce goods and services at a rate faster than the rate of increase in population. The problem, however, is complicated by the fact that an increase in population brings immediate demands for goods and services but does not immediately add up to an increase in actual working hours.

In any society not everyone works. In the American economy this can be said for three out of every five persons. Keep in mind the fact that we have virtually outlawed child labor, that people retire earlier, and that they live longer in their retirement. Added to this situation is the fact that the workweek has decreased by one-third in the past seventy years. And the trend continues toward more holidays, longer vacations, and, in general, fewer working hours during the calendar year.

PRODUCTIVITY

The basic answer to the problem of providing more goods and services for a growing population with a shrinking proportion of labor is *productivity*. This term describes the output of goods and services by each worker during each working hour, using the technology and tools available. Productivity explains how we increase quantities of wanted goods and services by insuring that the greatest return is obtained from the natural resources, labor, and capital used in their production. To put it even more plainly, productivity means that we must *efficiently* use all the factors of production.

Measuring productivity is more easily achieved in manufacturing processes than in service occupations. For example, five men working 40 hours in a watch factory may turn out 3,000 watches. This means that 200 hours (5×40) will be divided into 3,000 giving an output per man-hour of 15 watches. Any improvement in efficiency that will increase the rate of output from 15 watches will represent an increase in productivity. However, in the case of nurses, doctors, teachers, policemen, and other service groups the measurement of productivity raises certain obvious difficulties.

PRODUCTIVITY: FARM AND FACTORY

In the case of farming, such aids as fertilizers, insecticides, chemical weed killers, and new machines have increased productivity to such an extent in the years from 1947–1967 that farm output per hour in the United States almost tripled. Mechanical cotton pickers, for instance, now harvest more than 90 percent of Mississippi's cotton crop. Where used, they have replaced human cotton pickers who earned as little as $6 a day. So spectacular has technology's aid been to the farmer that since 1929 total farm output has almost doubled, while the farm population, as a percentage of the total population, has dropped from 25.1 to 5.5 percent! A glance at the accompanying chart shows that these shifts have continued during the past decade.

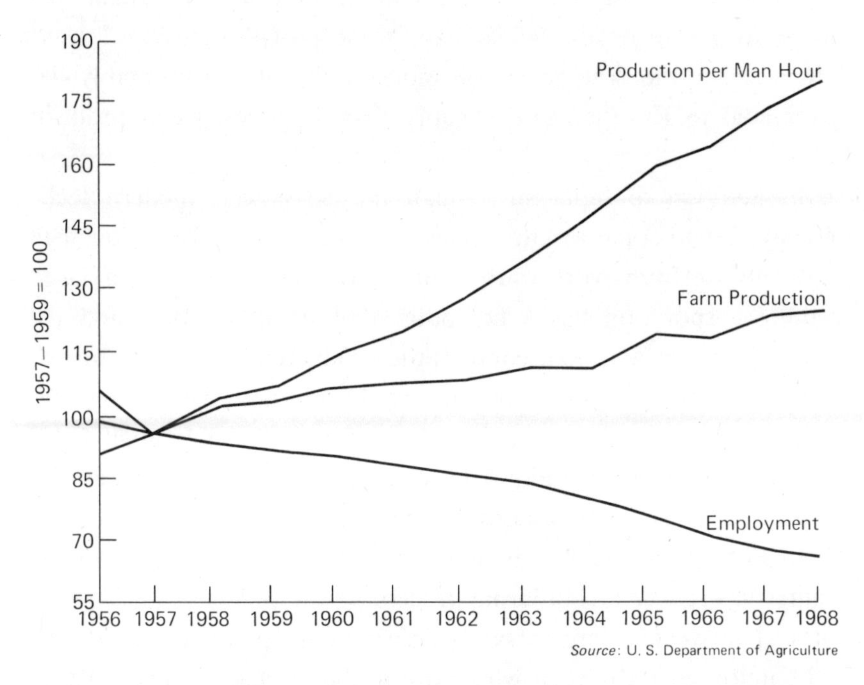

Fig. 2. Farm employment and production. (See also appendix table 1.)

Technological improvements (the application of knowledge to practical purposes such as the development of new machines and new methods) are not confined, of course, to the farm. In recent years the American economy has been growing at the rate of 4 percent a year. If this continues, the output of goods and services will, thanks to advances in technology, double in 18 years, triple in 28, quadruple in 35. (We should give additional thanks to the power of compound interest!)

Industry too has its share of mechanical marvels and miraculous methods of improving output per man-hour. A "push-button miner" cuts and loads up to 266 tons of coal an hour in one continuous operation. This mechanical giant, standing three stories high and weighing more than 1.5 million pounds, adds fantastically to the output of its three remote-control attendants. Other machines have almost tripled the amount of coal that a man can move in one day. So efficient have these post-World War II machines made the American coal industry that it can profitably deliver coal to Europe more cheaply than Europeans can produce it!

In addition to replacing human muscle power, modern technology can to some extent replace human brain power. Machines not only perform work, but control work as well. Thus a large baking corporation has a computer that handles orders and inventory and, in addition, controls the production process. It mixes, bakes, cooks, ices, quick-freezes, packages, and then stores the cakes in a fully automated warehouse the size of a football field. During the entire operation, the computer continually checks the processes and issues thousands of commands per second.

In Pittsburgh, the Westinghouse Electric Corporation computer center has reduced its ordering processes from 3–5 days to 4.5 minutes. The world's largest synthetic ammonia plant operates with 32 employees, only 21 of whom are in the worker category. Tape-controlled machine tools do the work of highly skilled machinists in many metal-working industries. A basic oxygen furnace produces steel 6 to 8 times faster than the traditional open-hearth method.

While some of these examples are admittedly extraordinary, the fact is that the use of new materials, new equipment, and new production methods is sufficiently widespread in American industry to account for the increased productivity necessary for higher living standards. That productivity is increasing can readily be seen from a glance at the record. From 1909 to 1947 output per man-hour grew at an annual rate of 2 percent; between 1947 and 1965 it rose 3.2 percent per year. The fact that the rate of increased productivity is not evenly distributed in these averages, however, should be pointed out. A recent Department of Commerce study of 70 industries, for example, revealed that the productivity of the most efficient plants was from 2 to 10 times greater than that of the least efficient ones.

Indications are that the increased productivity rate will be nourished by a number of recent developments. For one thing, technological change has been speeded up. The elapsed time between a new discovery and its commercial introduction has been reduced from an average of 37 years (around the 1900s) to 20 years before the change is adopted by 90 percent of the ultimate users. Total expenditures for research and development have almost quadrupled in a little more than 10 years. Federal government spending along these lines for *one* year now exceeds the total amount spent from the nation's very beginnings to the end of World War II. (Federal programs include special support for science education and the State Technical Services Act of 1965, which sponsors programs to acquaint local businesses with the latest technology and managerial techniques.) Scientists and engineers devoting their time to research and development have more than doubled in number since 1954. Through trade journals, scientific publications, and conferences, information about the new technology receives wider and more systematic coverage than ever before.

Above all, there exists a tremendous receptivity and adaptability on the part of management for innovation—changes that contribute to economic development. Management welcomes new and different ways of combining and utilizing resources in order to reduce costs, increase income, and raise profits. The aim is always the same: to obtain more units of output from the same resources or to obtain the same output with the use of fewer resources. Judging from the graph, this aim has been eminently successful; output has increased fourfold in the past 60 years.

NEED FOR INCREASED PRODUCTIVITY

Increased productivity helps to create an improved standard of living by ultimately contributing to lower prices for the consumer.

As a rule, there also will be greater profits for the businessman, and hence more spending in the economy and more tax revenue for the government.

Through increased productivity, workers also are able to enjoy increased leisure. Wages in industries with high rates of productivity are generally better than those in less efficient industries. In general, tedious, repetitious, and fatiguing tasks are more easily eliminated by improved technology.

Unfortunately, in the short run there is also a price for techno-

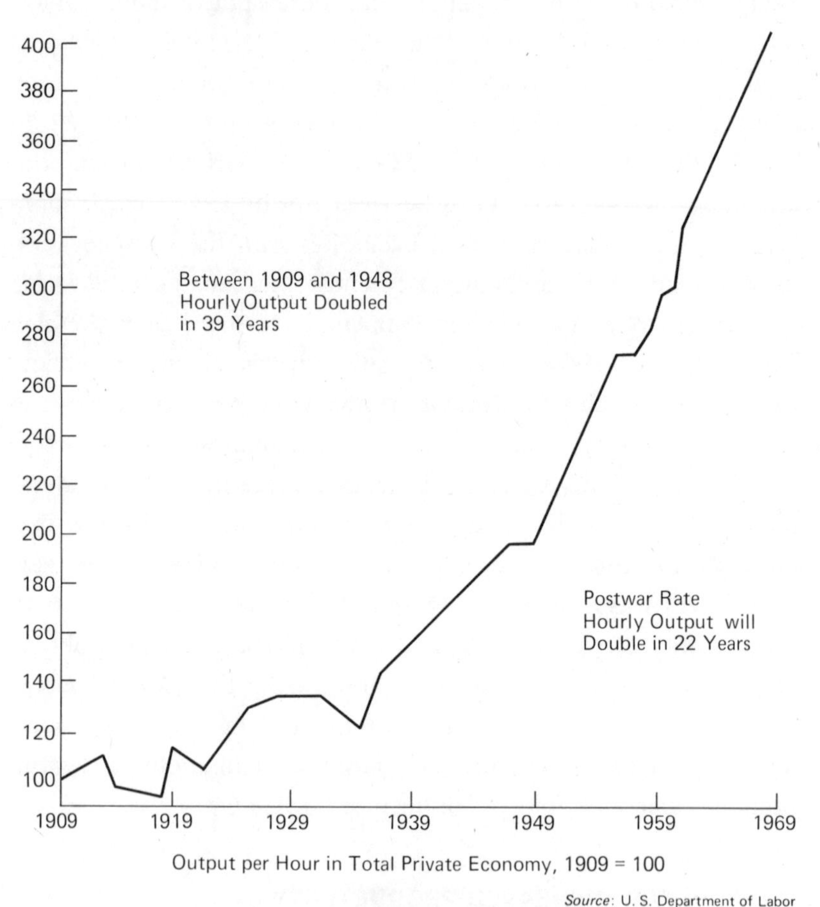

Fig. 3. How productivity has climbed.

logical progress. Technological unemployment—man displaced by machines—is occasionally a serious problem in some industries. Many unskilled jobs are often eliminated by labor-saving technology. Thousands of miners, trapped in towns where coal mining is the only industry, have encountered persistent economic difficulties. Millions of small farm owners, sharecroppers, tenant farmers, and hired hands, many of them Negroes, have been replaced by farm machines and have been forced into a migratory farmer status or have fled to the cities and become marginal workers. If a worker's skill is no longer needed, the individual (particularly if he is an older worker) may encounter great difficulty in finding another job. Though cold statistics of long-range economic progress are small comfort to a displaced worker, the fact remains that increased productivity ultimately makes it possible for more people to be employed at better wages in good times and to be cared for in bad times.

Why There Is High Productivity in the United States

At this point we might well ask why the United States is so productive and why its productivity rate is so high. By now it should be obvious that any explanation will involve the use to which it puts its resources: its land and natural resources, its capital, and especially its labor and its entrepreneurship (that enterprising and ingenious skill—or art—which continually seeks out a better way of doing the job).

Land resources that may be used for productive purposes total some 2 billion acres. One-fourth of this area is fertile cropland. Pasture land for livestock grazing comprises another one-half. (Some of this land, if needed, could be converted into cropland.) Valuable timberland adds almost another fourth.

In natural resources, with the possible exception of the Soviet Union, we are unrivaled in the sheer range of rich deposits of such vital minerals as iron ore, coal, limestone, and petroleum. Our energy resources are abundant: water power, coal, natural gas, and petroleum provide physical power. While we are not rich in fissionable materials, a good start has been made in developing nuclear energy.

In its capital resources, the United States without question leads the rest of the world in its store of man-made goods. It is roughly estimated that on the average each production worker is supported by some $20,000 in capital goods. In certain industries, such as gas and oil, the investment per worker may go as high as $200,000.

American labor brings to productivity a high degree of technical know-how and education. Labor also has a marked ability to adjust to frequent changes in production methods. It should be evident, too, that America has not lacked the "creative genius" of entrepreneurs, who organized the necessary capital and manpower to develop productive enterprises.

Importance of Saving and Investment

Fortified by these rich natural and human resources, the United States has been able to do the *saving* and *investment* necessary to increase its productivity. A simple tenet of economics tells us that savings from current production must be channeled into investment for future progress. Earliest man had to learn that some seed grain had to be saved for future crops; that to perpetuate his herd of sheep, he could not slaughter the entire flock. Under no economic system can you consume your entire stock of goods and still expect to have something left for future use.

In the United States the private citizen is free to save or not to save. He is free to determine the amount of his savings and the institution where he will place them: banks, stock exchanges, or insurance companies. In turn, they will invest the savings in various businesses, which will use them to purchase capital goods. (Investment, as economists use the term, refers to business decisions, not personal ones about whether to put one's money in stocks or real estate.) Business enterprises also save for investments; these funds come from retained profits not passed on to stockholders and from special tax allowances permitted for depreciation. The process of diverting part of an economy's current product for the creation of capital is referred to as capital formation.

New construction, additional machines, or replacement of worn-out or obsolete equipment (depreciation), and additions to inventories comprise capital formation. Increased productivity demands increased capital formation, both for increased needs and for the replacement of depreciated machinery.

TYPES OF BUSINESS OWNERSHIP

In order to organize productivity it is necessary that a firm be established to direct the many activities that its particular business demands. Here is the basic production unit where business decisions are made in a free enterprise economy. There are three types of business enterprise: individual ownership, partnership, and corporation. Together they add up to more than 11 million firms in the United States. They vary in size from the news stand where you get your morning paper to the American Telephone and Telegraph Company, which controls nearly all the country's telephones. They also differ, as we shall see, in their legal status, depending upon whether or not they are incorporated.

Individual ownership (or proprietorship) is perhaps best categorized by the desire to be "my own boss." This mean that the 9 million proprietorships (4 million of whom are farmers) enjoy all the advantages of running their businesses without interference from others, except of course to comply with legal requirements. (In some cases this means acquiring a special license.) Since relatively little capital and "red tape" are required for opening an individual business (usually retail shops or professional enterprises), this is considered the easiest type of business to enter.

Though being one's own boss may be psychologically satisfying and uncomplicated as far as decision-making and dividing the profits is concerned, there are obvious shortcomings. No one individual possesses all talents: a good designer may not be a good salesman; a good chef does not have the time to greet the customers. The life of the business lasts only as long as the life of the individual owner. Capital may be increased only with difficulty, since its accumulation depends solely upon one individual. Perhaps the greatest disadvantage is the matter of unlimited liability. In an individual ownership no distinction between business and personal property is made. If a firm fails, the individual is personally liable and may lose his home, automobile, or other valuable property to pay the business debts.

A partnership is a business association of two or more individuals. There are about 900,000 of these businesses, and about 1,500,000 corporations in the United States. Like the proprietorship, it is simple in its business arrangement, and indeed resembles it in many vital respects. A verbal or written agreement binds one partner to the decisions of all. This means that if one partner commits the firm to the purchase of an expensive piece of equipment, all partners are committed to its payment. If the bill cannot be met and the firm fails, all parties are personally liable for debts. For both proprietorships and partnerships the mortality record during the first year is extremely high. More than 90 percent of these failures, it is estimated, are due to some basic fault of management: incompetence, inexperience, undercapitalization.

In this respect the partnership resembles a proprietorship in having unlimited liability. It also has a limited life: the death or retirement of a single partner legally ends the business. Hence partnerships share with proprietorships a common difficulty in obtaining funds for long-range projects. Needless to say, however, the fact that there are more sources of income in a partnership gives it a wider latitude for gathering funds.

Partnerships also benefit from their ability to draw together diverse talents. This undoubtedly explains their popularity among professionals such as doctors, lawyers, and accountants. Specialists in different branches of medicine can team up and practice as a group. A trial lawyer can get together with one who specializes in writing briefs.

While talents may blend, temperaments often may not. Two heads may not be better than one; many voices may lead to dissent and dissolution. There can be little doubt that incompatibility is a big factor in partnership turnover. Some partnerships, it should be added, are expressly formed for only a limited time. Both proprietorships and partnerships, provided they are able to prosper and grow, find that extended growth brings with it another set of problems connected with expansion, problems that they are basically not so well equipped to handle as the more impersonal corporation.

Corporations: The Dominant Business Form

While the number of corporations and partnerships in the country is somewhat close, their influence on the economy is not. One corporation alone, the American Telephone and Telegraph Company, for instance, has more than 3 million shareholders holding more than 536 million shares, and earns an annual net income of more than $2 billion. Two-thirds of the nation's productive assets are owned by 500 corporations, which turn out two-thirds of the non-agricultural output.

Corporations may be used for any size business, but their great financial strength, their easy availability to credit for growth and expansion, and the pooling of talent make them indispensable for big business. Regardless of their size, corporations are considered legal "persons" created by law. This privilege in the form of a charter is granted by a state upon a firm's application. The charter enables the corporation to sue and be sued, borrow money, enter into contracts, and engage in practices common to any business enterprise.

As a legal "artificial person," the corporation enjoys continuity.

Contracts may be negotiated beyond the life expectancy of any of its owners, because the corporation's legal existence is not tied to any owner or manager. In fact, ownership may easily be transferred, either during an owner's lifetime or by his heirs, without disturbing the firm. In addition, the corporation enjoys limited liability. If the business fails, a stockholder (a part owner of the firm) loses whatever he paid for his shares of stock, but unlike the proprietorship or partnership, his personal property may not be taken to make up business losses. A well-established corporation with a good reputation also finds it easier to raise money by the sale of stocks and bonds. It can more easily borrow from banks than the other types of firms we mentioned.

MANAGING AND FINANCING THE CORPORATION

Management and ownership, especially in the larger corporations, are largely separated. Stockholders usually know little or nothing about the business beyond expecting to receive dividends (profits) and hoping to sell their shares at a higher price. Each share of stock entitles its owner to one vote, but stockholders seldom take the trouble to attend meetings at which the board of directors is elected. Generally they sign over their voting authority (proxies) to others. In turn, the board of directors appoints the company's officers, who do the actual management. Even if management owns shares of stock in a large corporation, their proportion of shares is usually so small that they represent only a tiny fraction of the total ownership.

This separation of ownership and control may lead to control by a few powerful insiders, whose actions may not always be in the best interests of the stockholders. The large corporation also tends to become impersonal in its many relations with customers and with its own working force. It may thus lose some of the advantages of bigness by wasteful and inefficient procedures. Double taxation may be a problem if profits already taxed are distributed to shareholders, who will then pay personal income taxes on these dividends.

How do corporations finance their expansion needs? Basically, four sources of funds are involved: stocks, bonds, corporate savings, and, of course, commercial banks.

Stock certificates are issued and sold to an investment bank, which sells them to the public. A company may print a *par value* on a stock. This represents an amount the company thinks the stock is worth when it is issued. Market value is usually a better indication of what the stock is really worth, for it is the price that investors in the open market are willing to pay for it.

Bonds represent debts of the corporation. A bondholder thus is not considered an owner, but rather a creditor of the firm. Bondholders receive a fixed rate of interest while holding bonds and a full return of their loan on the specified date of maturity. In case of bankruptcy, they are entitled to first claim, after the government, on the corporation's remaining assets.

Corporate savings represent the profits that are set aside after dividends are paid. In recent years this form of internal financing has become most common among large corporations. There are obvious savings in interest, since corporate savings do not involve bondholders. Furthermore, no additional stock (with additional dividends, and more votes) need be issued.

FEATURES OF A MARKET SYSTEM

Whether a firm is a proprietorship, a partnership, or a corporation, it operates within the framework of the American mixed free enterprise system. There is basic agreement on the main features of this system: private property, individual initiative of entrepreneurs, profits, competition, consumer choice, prices, and a role for government.

PRIVATE PROPERTY

A market society recognizes the right of individuals and private groups to own private property. This can be either personal property such as a house, or property concerned with the means of production, such as a factory. Thus there is freedom to own natural resources and capital and to use them in production. This right, like any right, is not without limitations. Provided suitable compensation is made, the government has the legal right to confiscate private property for the general welfare. For example, if a person's house is in an area through which a road is planned, the government reserves the right to take over the property—provided proper legal action is taken and compensation is given. Or during wartime, automobile manufacturers may be required to stop producing pleasure cars and, instead, turn out tanks, jeeps, and army trucks.

Individual Initiative

Individual initiative by entrepreneurs is basic to the operation of the market system. This initiative includes a range of decisions as simple as that made by a newsboy concerning his delivery route to such weighty ones as those made by an electric utility company in building an atomic reactor. Business decisions mainly revolve around the problem of seeking increased profits by attempting to produce most cheaply those goods that consumers most want.

Profits

If producers are successful in their sales, they will receive profits. Profits are the returns to a business from sales after the operating expenses have been subtracted. Naturally, profits are possible only if consumers will buy a businessman's products at prices that more than cover his expenses. In a sense, profits represent a reward for the risks taken by the businessman. These risks, it may be added, include the possibility of losses instead of profits and, even worse, being forced to close down the business entirely. Profits may be considered payment for the services performed by a businessman in running his enterprise. They also include a return to investors for the use of their savings. Profits in a market system are powerful incentives for businessmen to conduct productive enterprises. The profit motive thus permits individuals engaged in economic activities to seek to obtain maximum money incomes.

Competition

Prices are kept within reasonable bounds by competition. Rival individual or corporate enterprises continually seek to win customers to buy their products or services. In the process of seeking greater profits, competitors seek individual customers either by lowering their prices (but keeping in mind the need for profits), by advertising their superior virtues, or by offering better quality, styling, or services than their competitor. Competition among buyers and sellers is encouraged in order to assure the more efficient production of goods and services. Freedom of choice in producing and buying commodities is a most important ingredient in the competitive system.

Consumer Choice

Consumer choice is a vital factor in determining what individuals and corporations will produce. Needless to say, this choice is not the fancy-free one of a child in front of a candy store. For not only does consumer choice reflect tastes and appetites but to be significant in the economy it must also be based upon incomes and the prices of the goods and services offered to the consumer.

Prices

Prices are the "messengers" of the economy that carry decisions from consumers to producers. Buyers and sellers in countless markets for innumerable goods and services make decisions based upon prices—favorable or unfavorable, to buy or not to buy, to sell or not to sell. Eventually the decisions of consumers, based upon prices, will determine what is produced in a private enterprise economy.

Government

While there is comparatively little government ownership in the economy, there is a significant area reserved for government intervention. Hence we find government responsible for setting policies for the nation's vital money and credit system. Individuals are free to enter into business contracts, which are enforceable by the courts. Government also has a major role in maintaining the market system by protecting private property and by encouraging effective competition. Where firms attempt to prevent competition, the government has the power to enforce laws that will compel them to abandon practices that stifle trade. In addition, government provides for the health, education, and welfare of the people, and it has the responsibility for seeing that the economy grows and remains on an even keel.

Later chapters will explain fully this brief description of our price-directed economy and critically evaluate this system. Before we do this, however, we must examine in greater detail our market system so that we may arrive at a fuller understanding of how resources are allocated and distributed. In other words, how do we apply our productive resources and facilities to specific use, in view of the many alternative uses to which they might be put? And how do people get the many items that are finally produced?

CHAPTER 3

THE MARKET SYSTEM

Allocating and Distributing Resources

Perhaps the greatest challenge faced by the United States economy is that of making its market system continue to operate efficiently. The market system is the method our price-directed, profit-motivated economy has evolved for producing and distributing goods. The market system determines what a businessman will produce and how he will produce it in response to prices and the costs of the items that enter into the production of goods and services: land, capital, raw materials, and labor. The market system also explains why consumers decide to buy the products that business offers for sale, and it further explains how businessmen generally produce only that which they can produce and sell at a profit.

THE MARKET SYSTEM

The market system has been described as an "efficient, impartial, and automatic control" for the production and distribution of goods and services. A market is a way of doing business that permits buyers and sellers of related items, such as the fabric market with its great variety of fabrics made from different fibers, to deal with each other. A telephone, a supermarket, the mail, the stock exchange, or a commodity exchange (where a product like cocoa is traded) can be a market. Thus the market system provides a type of economic communications network that links the buying and selling decisions of millions of individual buyers and sellers.

Furthermore, the market system is impersonal because it relies on the forces of supply and demand (about which we shall have more to say shortly). In turn, supply and demand help to establish a system of prices for goods and services. Prices dictate and bring together the millions of separate, individual decisions into a sort of economic vote. In this type of balloting we may discover that most people consider 45 cents for a loaf of bread too high a price, but that bakers may feel that 20 cents a loaf is too low for them.

It might be wise to take a further look at this competitive market system to discover the key as to how consumers hope to obtain goods at the lowest prices, how producers hope to obtain the greatest profits, and how workers hope to secure better jobs at highest wages. How are these seemingly contradictory aims adjusted in a system that is basically unplanned, and where everyone seeks his own private satisfaction?

MODEL OF A MARKET SYSTEM

To answer these questions we must provide a model of the market system. Now a model is simply an attempt to construct a common pattern of uniformity out of many scattered facts. It is a generalization that springs from previous experience. By virtue of its few simple features, a model is to a great extent an artificial creation. It serves, however, as a substitute for reality, enabling one to see clearly the workings of economic theory and to determine how the actual economic world varies from the theory.

In the model of a competitive market system, for instance, the businessman produces goods and services in the hope that he will make a profit. Consumers, backed by money, "vote" for these goods and services through their purchases. Economic votes and the amounts of goods and services available on the market interact and determine prices and the further production of goods and services. Businessmen will continue to respond to consumer demand by producing more goods if they find it profitable to do so. They will attempt to increase their productivity by combining the resources used in producing their goods in the most efficient way they know in order to make greater profits (particularly in industries where products are most sought after). To obtain resources, businessmen compete for land, capital, natural resources, labor, and entrepreneurship. The owners of these resources thus obtain incomes that reflect their particular contribution to production. With these incomes they can then buy desired goods and services. Competing as they do with others, businessmen, again, are under pressures of price competition to use resources most efficiently. Above all, in this market economy, the price of goods is affected by the interplay of demand and supply.

Here too, we can construct a simple model that will illustrate how the forces of demand and supply direct prices in the market.

DEMAND AND SUPPLY

Demand, in the language of the economist, refers to the amounts of a particular product or service that consumers would buy at various prices at particular times. Consumers at times will buy more of a product at a lower price than they will at a higher price. Additional satisfactions can be obtained if the price of goods drops sufficiently. More people can now afford the product. Since everyone loves a bargain, a lowered price tends to stimulate people to stock up for their needs or wants. This will be most evident for goods with many uses that can readily be substituted for higher-priced products. An example that comes quickly to mind is the increased buying at lower prices of margarine, which may be substituted for oil in baking or frying, or for butter or preserves as a spread.

Tastes, Income, Prices of Other Goods

At any point in time, demand for a product depends upon: (1) *Tastes.* This is broad category that deals with one's basic attitude towards a particular item. "One man's meat is another man's poison" is an indicator that tells us that some people will choose a winter vacation over a summer one, red over green, mod fashions over more traditional ones, or potatoes over rice. Then, too, decisions as to whether or not an item is a luxury or a necessity will influence demand. (2) *Income.* Obviously a buyer's income and the amount he is willing to spend influence the amount of a good that can be bought at various prices. (3) *Prices of other goods.* The prices and availability of substitute products (margarine for butter) also affect demand of a specific good. Complementary goods (those used together) affect each other's demand. An increase in the price of automobiles might cause a decrease in the demand for tires.

Using turkey as an illustration, let us see how price would affect the *demand* for the product.

A glance at this demand schedule indicates the total market for turkeys and illustrates the point that more turkeys will be sold at a lower price.

Demand for Turkey	
At a price per pound of	Consumers willing to buy
$ .59	10,000
.54	10,500
.49	11,000
.44	11,500
.39	12,000

Now let us examine the producers' side, supply. Here we are talking about the amount of a particular item or service offered for sale at various prices at a particular time. As with the previous schedule, let us use turkey as our illustration.

Supply of Turkey	
At a price per pound of	Producers willing to supply
$ .39	10,000
.44	10,500
.49	11,000
.54	11,500
.59	12,000

It comes as no surprise to discover that more turkeys will be offered at higher prices than at lower prices. Higher prices permit profitable production while lower prices reduce or even eliminate profits. Shifts in supply depend on the cost of production, including, of course, the cost of resources used and the particular technology of production.

Market Price

If we now look back to the demand schedule for turkey, we see that more turkeys would be sold at 39 cents per pound than at any other price. But a glance at the supply schedule reveals that producers would be willing to supply the greatest number at 59 cents. Obviously consumers and producers have some basic differences here. However, if we examine both schedules at the 49-cent price, we discover that 11,000 birds will be both demanded and offered. This interaction of supply and demand is known as market price—the price at which the amount consumers are willing to pay equals the amount at which producers are willing to sell.

Changes in supply and demand occur for the reasons already cited. If supply increases and demand remains the same, more of the product will be sold at a lower market price. Increased demand, if supply stays the same, will see more of the product sold at a higher market price.

Elasticity

Demand also varies according to what economists like to call its *elasticity*. This term refers to how much of an increase or decrease there will be in the amount demanded if the price is lowered or raised by a given figure. Thus the price for wheat is said to be inelastic because a reduction in price does not encourage people to eat more bread; hence there will not be a change in the amount of wheat demanded. Usually the demand for necessities tends to be inelastic.

On the other hand, the demand for luxuries, or goods readily substituted, tends to be elastic. Steaks are in the elastic-demand category. A lowering of price will encourage more people to buy them. An increase in price will discourage buyers. In other words, the quantity demanded will vary greatly following a change in price.

Knowledge of the elasticity of demand will go far toward providing an understanding of consumer demand and what and how much will be produced. It will help to explain further the forces of demand and supply—how prices result from the combined decisions of individual consumers to buy and of individual producers to sell.

Elasticity of demand also will be useful in shedding light on the "farm problem." Some of the farmers' basic products, as we indicated, are price inelastic. (Remember, they do not readily respond to price changes.) Wheat production, stimulated by a tremendous technological revolution, has increased its productivity so much that output per acre and output per man-hour keep rising steadily. While the output for this crop increases, demand has tended to grow slowly. Increased population accounts for an increase in demand but individuals, as we noted, do not eat more bread, even when their incomes rise. Inelastic demand for wheat thus tends to fall behind its rapidly increasing supply. Surpluses thus pile up and prices drop down. Faced with this problem, farmers have turned to the government for relief from the difficulties in the competitive free market. Government price supports and other controls have been introduced to help the farmer allocate his products in a way that will return him a greater income. Other "solutions" for preventing the oversupply involve governmental or private price setting.

Judging from this example of the farm problem it would seem that there must exist other irregularities in the "perfect market"; that the model of the market economy in reality must vary considerably from the "pure" competition of the price-directed economy. Since we have repeatedly referred to the fact that the American economy is "mixed," with a considerable element of government incorporated into its movements, this situation should come as no surprise. In addition, giant corporations and giant unions have made the "pure" capitalist model even more remote from today's economic realities. But even though pure competition rarely exists because of the many imperfections in the market system, changes in price still remain the main regulators of economic activity in the American economy. Changes in price, however, increasingly are set by standards of imperfect competition, by producers commanding positions powerful enough to influence the market. Under these conditions prices are often artificially set and as a result resources are frequently wasted and profits pushed out of line.

Before we explore the imperfections further, perhaps it might be well to review briefly the ideal competitive market system. Business produces goods and services hoping to make a profit. Backed by money, consumers vote for goods and services. The interaction of consumer demand and of producers' supply determines the production of goods and services and their prices. Competition forces businessmen, in order to make a profit, to use resources efficiently. Owners of resources receive income in proportion to their contribution to production.

CRITICISMS OF A MARKET SYSTEM

Generally any discussion of the imperfections of the market system revolves around three major criticisms: (1) it neglects nonprofit goods and services; (2) it depends essentially on rational behavior of producers and consumers; and (3) it does not function properly when prices are manipulated.

Since the market considers only private costs and private gains, community costs and community gains may differ. It may be cheaper for private enterprise to produce under conditions that will pollute the air and streams, thus creating a conflict between private gain and public well-being. Communities also frown upon undesirable types of production, such as those involving habit-forming drugs. Some social goods and services do not respond to the competition of the market: police and fire protection, national defense, parks, highways, mass education, and urban renewal projects. There also are the unfortunates, the sick and crippled, the needy, the misfits, the unemployed, and the indigent aged who cannot manage the rigors of the competitive market system. Society steps in here and offers a helping hand. Adam Smith, the father of the theory of the marketplace, said that a man "by pursuing his own interest frequently promotes that of the society more effectually than when he really intends to promote it." Today's realities have greatly modified this doctrine!

Rational behavior, unfortunately, is not in such common supply as to meet all the demands of the market system. Individuals acting for their own interests, as the market assumes they will, do not always act correctly. Consumers and producers frequently act illogically, if not stupidly. Consumers and producers, for example, are not always aware of the existence of needed products, or how these products perform. Annually thousands of businesses fail, the majority of them because of poor management. Consumers particularly are often ignorant of how the performance of many products rates against possible substitutes. Glamorous, emotional, or otherwise irrelevant appeals by some advertisers also contribute toward the creation of ill-informed consumers.

MANAGING PRICES: MONOPOLISTIC PRACTICES

The market does not function properly when prices are manipulated. For one thing, there is a considerable amount of nonprice competition in today's market. Economic rivalry is not always fought with lower prices. In the case of the automobile industry, emphasis is usually placed on changes in design and style, rather than on lower prices. The makers of soda pop keep turning out the same ginger ale but decide to bottle it in a "new and improved" container. Advertising may be used instead of price as a competitive weapon. In the case of cigarettes, the products may be quite similar but each company hopes by advertising to fix its brand name in the public's mind. Then people will ask for *their* product rather than any other. In each of these cases cited, the manufacturer was attempting to make his product so different in its appeal that it would be in a class by itself. In other words, consumers are asked not to think of the supply at many prices and of many brands, but to demand only the unique or imaginary advantages of a specific brand.

Perfect competition calls for an identical product sold by a large number of sellers. When the entire supply is produced by a few large competitors, the situation is referred to as oligopoly. Monopoly exists when the entire supply of the product is controlled by one seller who sets the price. When monopoly exists to an appreciable degree society cannot depend on the market to bring about the most effective allocation of resources in response to consumers' demands. Monopoly makes it possible for a business to increase its profit by selling a smaller quantity of its product at a higher price. It does this by restricting production to the level that will bring the greatest return to the company. Even though the monopolist could take in more money by turning out more goods at a lower price, he prefers to turn out fewer goods at a higher price. He is particularly likely to do this where he controls an essential product and there are no substitutes available.

Under monopolistic competition a limited number of producers sell products slightly differentiated. This is particularly true in the automobile industry where Ford, Chrysler, and General Motors sell similar cars in various price lines. Among these competitors, however, there are little or no price differentials for particular lines. Generally the presence of only a few big sellers is conducive to the growth of monopolistic situations. This problem has come to the fore with the rise of big business. Big business, it must be remembered, resulted from advantages of low-cost mass production. Products, it was discovered, could be made and distributed widely and cheaply by concentrating men and machinery in large-scale operations. Such mass production contributed greatly to present high living standards. It also helped to foster monopolistic competition and its related problems among giant producers in such industries where there are requirements for enormous capital outlays, such as automobiles, steel, aluminum, and electrical equipment.

Competition among big businessmen is sometimes avoided by attempts to form associations with other big businessmen to influence prices. Since it is often difficult for the smaller companies in that same industry to fight back with lower prices, they usually follow the leaders. Generally it is more possible to influence prices in industries that require large amounts of capital (automobile and steel) than in industries where the investment is smaller (clothing and candy making). The greater the investment needed to enter an industry, the fewer will be the number of companies in that industry, and the fewer the number of companies, the easier it is to get together to influence prices. Labor unions, too, have as their purpose the avoidance of individual bargaining in the market's demand for labor. By controlling the supply of labor, unions hope to overcome the competitive market forces that could lower wages.

Not all big businesses, it must be emphasized, engaged in monopolistic competition necessarily hurt the consumer. Indeed, some of them, like the nationwide grocery chains, have invaded local markets where little competition previously prevailed and the result actually has been increased competition. (Paradoxically, antitrust actions have recently been taken against food chains, such as the A & P, whose size and efficiency permit them to undersell the local grocer!) However, the factors that bring about big business and permit us to enjoy its advantages of mass production (better products and service, greater variety and lower prices) may also introduce abuses of a monopolistic nature. Beyond a certain point, the advantages of large-scale production do not continue. Increased bigness may merely become a threat to competition. The Justice Department has recently evinced an interest in this threat due to the mushrooming of giant conglomerates. The question to be decided is the degree to which these crazy-quilt assemblages of companies in unrelated industries affect the traditional workings of the American competitive system.

Competition may be difficult to maintain because expensive technology may eliminate small-scale producers. A new process, a patented product, or a copyrighted item may put competitors in the economic shadows. Fair trade laws, which encourage price fixing by the manufacturer in retail trade, also may reduce competition. Then, too, the existence of a large national market encourages mass marketing and economic concentration at the expense of small competitors.

Where a monopolistic situation is maintained, it relies upon continued control of the market and the ability to keep possible newcomers out of the market. For obviously, if enough competitors entered the market they would force prices down as they struggled for customers. Prices will be kept at the point where the consumer will be exploited but where the monopolist will make the largest profits. Profits thus often will be "out of line." Since production will be restricted to keep the output (down) to the point where profits are greatest, it follows that there also will be less employment. The existence of monopolistic situations also impairs the efficiency of the competitive economic system, especially in regard to the allocation of resources. Lacking the sharp stimulus of competition, the monopolist feels little or no need to improve his product or to attempt to cut his costs of production. In short, the monopolist is a drag on the self-regulating aspect of the market economy since he has chosen to be outside the law of supply and demand.

Limits to Monopolistic Prices

There are, of course, limits to the manipulating that monopolists may practice with higher prices and lower output. You cannot force people to buy if prices are too high, unless you are selling items they must have. Substitutes are generally available, plastics or aluminum for steel, for instance. Public opinion in a democratic nation remains a vital force for calling attention to abuses. Finally, there exist antitrust laws that specifically aim to insure competition and regulatory acts that attempt to prevent abuses in the market.

The Sherman Antitrust Act of 1890 fathered the attempt to prevent "restraint of trade" and to keep open the doors to competition. A generation later the Clayton Act and in 1950 the Celler

Anti-Merger Act further strengthened the original act. A Federal Trade Commission, established in 1914, helps to enforce the antitrust laws and the rules of fair competition. When necessary, the federal government through the Federal Trade Commission and the Antitrust Division of the Department of Justice takes cases to court to protect, promote, and preserve competition. The basic idea behind antitrust legislation is that competition is good and monopoly is bad. To enforce competition, the government may attempt to break up monopolistic businesses, or prosecute those that reduce competition by price agreements (such as the case, in 1961, of the 29 electrical equipment manufacturers who were convicted of a conspiracy to fix prices). In recent years government action has been concentrated in the attempt to discourage threats to competition at the very outset. Unfortunately, the problems of monopoly control are persistent. Fourscore years of antitrust legislation and prosecution have not prevented the continued growth of big business and ensuing monopolistic practices. The antitrust record, however, can claim some successes in containing mergers, eliminating some of the more flagrant forms of price and output fixing, and enforcing standards of fair competition that serve to keep the economy within reasonable bounds.

The 1960s, as we note in the graph, witnessed a large increase in the number of firms that merged or amalgamated, thus cutting down on competition. As a result, oligopoly (competition by a few large producers) is a significant factor in our market economy today. Thus the fundamental problem remains one of determining how to keep the benefits of a large-scale production through big business without running the risk of eliminating competition in our economy.

Public Utilities

Monopolies not only are permitted but are actively encouraged in the case of public utilities (services for electrical power, trans-

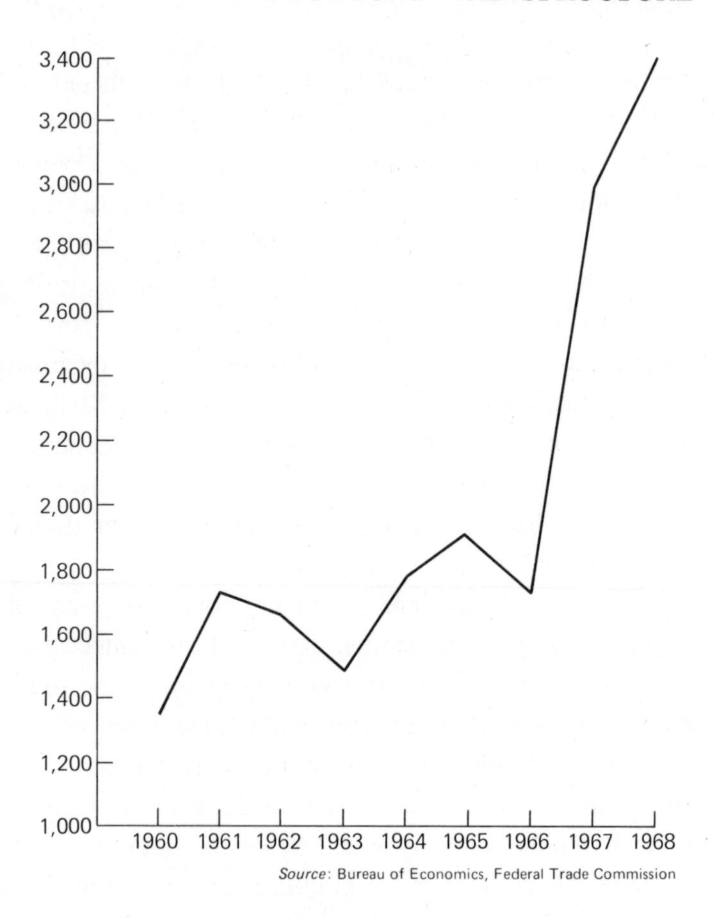

Fig. 4. Increase in business mergers.

portation, and communication). In return for monopoly privileges, public utilities are directly regulated by the government for the public's protection. The thought here is that essential services are involved; that large investments are necessary, as in the case of railroads and airlines; and that natural monopolies are present. (It would not be wise to have two competing electric companies cover the same territory. The wastes in ripping up streets and duplicating expensive capital equipment are obvious.) Commencing with the Interstate Commerce Act of 1887, the federal government regulated the railroad industry. In some cases all three levels of government own and operate public utilities: The federal government operates the Tennessee Valley Authority electrical grid; some states are in the transportation and electrical business; while municipal governments frequently operate their own transportation and water systems. Today the federal, state, and municipal governments fix the price, or prices, charged by industries "affected with a public service" and regulate the quality of the service or services provided. Determining fair prices and fair profits remains a difficult problem, however, in government regulation of public utilities.

GOVERNMENT AND THE ECONOMY

Thus, in certain areas of vital importance where competition would be wasteful, government decision-making is substituted for the decisions of the free market. Government participation in the economy, as previously indicated, has so modified our price-directed, free market system that the term "mixed economy" is used to describe the extent of the change. This participation takes three main routes: *regulating business, taxing and spending,* and *taking measures to keep the economy growing* (*and growing on an even keel*).

We have already seen how government seeks to regulate monopolistic practices and how it aims to maintain competition. We also noted how public utilities, in return for being "excused" from competition, are regulated as to rates charged and services provided. Federal farm programs whose purpose it is to limit the output of certain products such as wheat and cotton also can be cited. Familiar to all of us are varied regulations by all levels of government dealing with harmful or adulterated foods and medicines. Government ownership and operation of utilities, while not universal, is considerable on all levels.

Government taxing and spending have increased rapidly in the years since World War II. Changes in either category greatly affect business activity. By removing available cash, taxes influence consumer income and business profits. They remove spending power and transfer it to the government. The government is then in a position to spend it and affect the economy in various ways. In other words, the $500 you pay in taxes reduces your ability to buy consumer items such as a TV set and a refrigerator, but it increases by that same amount the government's ability to buy spacecraft and defense hardware or to build roads.

Taxes are high because government spending is high. Two-thirds of federal spending is connected in some way with national defense. Then, too, the increase in population—it almost doubled in the past 50 years—and the accompanying demands for increased services (education, Social Security, and health and welfare benefits) have added tremendously to the bill that taxes pay. Many of these services have long been operated by the government because they are not considered profitable for businessmen in the free market. There is great need for these services at reasonably low prices. It would be difficult, moreover, to determine prices for individual police or fire protection. Whether or not the government increases or decreases its economic role and in what order priorities are set are both determined by political votes in the light of certain social goals: economic growth, stability, security, freedom, and justice.

With growing populations we have growing urbanization and growing financial problems. State and local governments, with some help from the federal government, are actively engaged in combating costly problems of housing, crime, transportation, welfare, and education. Local and state expenses continue to rise at the rate of 10 percent a year. With their revenues failing to reach the nation's annual growth rate of 5 to 6 percent, President Nixon labeled their predicament a "fiscal mismatch". While cities watch their expenses mount through increased personnel and increased salaries, the Federal Government, by taxing these incomes, reaps additional revenues!

To ease the growing fiscal burden, President Nixon recently proposed a landmark revenue sharing plan under which states would receive "block grants" of federal monies with a "mandatory pass through" insuring proportional amounts to their cities. Local governments would receive sums based on revenues actually raised from their areas. These revenues would be in addition to existing federal grant-in-aid programs. Whether or not the legislation that finally emerges tallies with this outline, there seems to be little doubt that increased federal aid to states and cities will rise sharply in the coming years.

Taxing and spending used for these and other services represent a considerable participation in the nation's economy. The government purchases roughly one-fifth of the gross national product and taxes one-fourth of the annual national income! If the economy is running at capacity (full employment), government purchasing can have a powerful effect upon competition for the nation's scarce resources. In such a case the government can help bring about increased demand for the limited supply of goods, thus forcing prices up and possibly contributing to an inflationary situation.

Government is a major contributor to research and development (R & D). R & D assists in unraveling the mysteries of science and engineering and applying these results to the practical needs of the economy. New products, improved techniques, and increased productivity are frequent benefits from R & D. Although private industry performs 75 percent of all the research and development in the United States—the total bill was almost $17 billion in 1967—at least more than half of the cost was paid for by the federal government.

Finally, the government has a tremendous influence, as we will discover later, in deciding whether our economy continues to grow and whether it is able to keep prices from going too high (inflation) or business from falling into a slump (recession). Congress in 1946 passed the Employment Act that specifically gives the federal government responsibility for keeping the country prosperous and for seeing that general prices do not get too much out of line—too high or too low. Again, the federal government does this by taxing and spending and by the regulations we have observed. In addition, the government also exerts its influence by controlling our money system through the Federal Reserve System's power over commercial banks. This power, as we shall detail in a later chapter, is aimed at regulating the supply of bank credit (borrowing) as a means of influencing economic conditions.

THE MARKET TODAY

While the majority of economic decisions is still made by buyers and sellers in a competitive market system, considerable modification has been made in this system. Monopolistic competition plays an important role in today's markets. Government decisions, too, are extremely significant in deciding how productive resources will be used. To a considerable extent this important growth in government influence stems from attempts to correct the abuses and imperfections of the market.

With the growth of big business, big labor, and big government, we are challenged to examine the increasing difficulty of maintaining effective competition in many parts of our market economy. We are faced in such cases with the need to weigh the costs of preserving competition against the benefits to be derived from mass production in the hands of big business with a potential for monopolistic practices.

CHAPTER 4

DISTRIBUTING INCOME

A Fair Economy

INCOME

How do we distribute the output of the economic system we have been describing? Distribution is accomplished by means of *income* (expressed in terms of money), which represents what people obtain from their contributions to production. We are all familiar with income expressed as wages, salaries, rent, dividends, or profits. No matter what name you give "income," ultimately its source derives from production. Man's age-old problem of satisfying his wants, which continuously outrace his limited resources, thus is one of increasing his income by increasing economic growth: the output of goods and services. Under a free market system the highest incomes go to those whose productive resources—labor, raw materials, managerial talents, property, or funds—are in greatest demand. With these incomes they can acquire, according to their tastes and preferences, a larger share of the economy's goods and services. It follows that those whose resources are in least demand, or even unemployed, are in a poor position to accumulate income. Hence, they obtain a smaller share of the economy's output.

Why, then, are some skills or resources in a superior position to others in obtaining income? This is so because the actual amount of income each will receive is determined by the market for his particular service to production, a market greatly influenced by consumer demand for products using these services. If you are a carpenter looking for a good income it is sound, if hardly startling, advice that you will do better in the building or furniture industry than in the railroad industry. We therefore similarly can say that the market system sets the prices on the services of land, labor, and capital, determining wage rates, land rents, interest rates and profits.

As in other areas of economic activity, the market does not have sole control over the distribution of income. Government taxing and spending policies attempt to correct some of the injustices of the market by the redistribution of income. Through high taxation rates, money is taken from high-income groups and spent on veterans, the unemployed, old people, public housing, public schools, and welfare services that are mainly of benefit to people with lower incomes. In addition, such private groups as labor unions influence the distribution of income by their ability to control the supply of labor in a particular industry and thus raise wages above what they might be in the free market. Industries in positions of monopolistic control may attempt to fix their prices so that profits are higher than they would be under market conditions of supply and demand.

WHO GETS THE HIGHER INCOME?

But let us return to our basic question of why some skills or resources are more successful than others in obtaining higher incomes. Some examples are obvious to all: Individuals with outstanding talents such as atomic scientists, heart transplant surgeons, space scientists and engineers, and computer programmers have little competition in their fields of endeavor and hence can command extremely large salaries and fees. While these examples may strike you as unusual (and they are) nevertheless they emphasize the first principle of payment: Those who have skills and abilities that are in scarce supply and in great demand are better rewarded.

Skilled workers with their years of special training and experience receive more than unskilled laborers. Unskilled jobs, like sweeping, cleaning, and routine mechanical operations, are easily learned. It does not take long for new people to enter these ranks. Therefore there are many unskilled laborers who compete with one another. It follows that their wages must be lower than those whose specialized skills, like neurosurgeons and atomic physicists, make their number relatively limited, yet for whose services there are great demands.

There is another principle of determining income besides the matter of skills. *Those who are engaged in industries where the product or service is in great demand will generally earn greater incomes.* Engineers in the aircraft industries will probably command more money than those working in the railroad industry; one industry is booming, while the other is declining. Specialists in handling the laser, which has changed metal-working practices, and in solid-state circuitry, which has created big changes in the electronics industry, will earn some of today's highest salaries for they are in industries in which some of the greatest demands exist. When producers find their goods in great demand they are eager to obtain the best chemists, engineers, and other skilled workers. Because they are doing well in business, they are willing to compete in paying high salaries and wages for the skilled employees they need. If the workers are easily replaced, however, producers will pay lower prices, by comparison, for these services. In the United States, about 70 percent of all income goes to wages and salaries.

Inequality of Income

While a market system leaves the door open to improvements in the distribution of income, it acknowledges certain inequalities at the very outset. We are all aware that human beings vary greatly in their native abilities and that training and education help to intensify these differences. Individuals also possess different amounts of property, land and natural resources, savings, and stocks and bonds, all of which give them obvious income advantages. Many inherit fortunes, which not only provide income but permit them to start out on the quest for more income with all the benefits that money can provide.

As can easily be gathered, income distribution is a highly controversial area, involving the "haves" and "have nots" in questions of economic justice, taxation, and the redistribution of income. Less controversial, but just as important, is the influence of the distribution of income on the total economy. Thus, if the rich get richer and the poor get poorer, we know, from our knowledge of elastic and inelastic demand, that the demand for luxury goods will grow at the expense of necessities. As incomes rise, there is a tendency for proportionately more to be spent on luxuries than on necessities. A food bill for a family of four with an income of $3,000 may be $1,000 a year, or one-third of the income. On the other hand, $5,000 spent for food by a similar-sized family with an income of $25,000 represents only one-fifth of its income. A good deal of the remaining four-fifths will be spent on expensive clothes, motorboats, travel, cars, and luxury items. Indeed, statistics reveal that families with incomes over $10,000 are disproportionately heavy purchasers of books, hi-fi equipment, liquor, car rentals, and air travel. In other words, spending patterns that are based on income received will affect the size and type of the output of goods and services, and the size and type of employment. These changes in consumer demand can thus change the allocation of resources and hence influence the distribution of income. One producer compared himself to a cork "floating on the ocean, and the consumers are the waves that move the cork. Our job is to discern what they want and give it to them."

Income distribution is usually divided into two categories: functional and personal.

Functional Income

Functional income refers to the income earned according to one's role in the production of goods and services. Included here is income earned by employees, the self-employed, corporation executives, landlords, and bondholders.

Personal Income

Personal income is based upon the 60.5 million households in the United States. It includes all the income of all members of a family who, of course, may receive the varied types of income mentioned as functional income. Family incomes also are supplemented by part-time employment, which does not appear in personal income statistics. Welfare allowances, free lunches, food stamps, and subsidized rents, also may add to the family's real income. In the final analysis these items represent money or money that would have to be spent. Progressive income taxes are adjusted to take proportionately less from the lower-income groups. This helps to increase the disposable income (money left after paying all types of personal income taxes) of this group of income earners.

By any measure, including personal income, the United States economy is not only rich but is growing more so. Since World War II the pattern of income distribution has changed so much that $8,600 (1968 census) is now the median for family income. (This means that one-half of the families are to be found above this figure while the other half are below.) It is now estimated that about 13 million, or more than one-fourth of American families, are earning $10,000 or more a year, compared with 10 million or 17 percent in 1961. Interesting comparisons for income distribution in previous periods appear in the accompanying chart.

POVERTY AMIDST PLENTY

So marked is America's affluence that one congressman complained, "How do you make an individual who is earning nine

Percent of Families with Incomes in 1965 Dollars of:

1929
1955
1965
Over $10,000
6%
14%
$6–10,000
10%
23%
$4–6,000
16%
27%
31%
$2–4,000
38%
23%
19%
22%
17%
Under $2,000
30%
14%
10%

Adapted; Changing Profile of the Americal Economy, 1967, *Chase Manhattan Bank, New York*

Fig. 5. Distribution of families by income bracket. (See appendix table 2.)

or ten thousand dollars a year, has his house mortgage paid out, operates two cars, and is adding a boat, identify with the war on poverty?" And intolerable poverty continues to exist in a society that has succeeded in widely distributing an unprecedented prosperity. Family income, as mentioned, has increased since World War II, especially among wage earners and low-salaried clerical workers. Income increased among these groups mainly because of the great labor shortages of the war period, and the aid given by collective bargaining and minimum wage legislation. Since 1948 no great shifts have taken place in income distribution, but all levels of income, including that of the poor, have risen. Even the approximately one-eighth of the population who are classified as living in poverty have experienced a doubling in their income over the past generation or so. Incidentally, this group has decreased since 1961, when it made up 22 percent of the population.

In defining poverty, the government considers family size and age brackets for farm and nonfarm households. A family is "poor" if its income does not permit it to buy enough food, clothing, shelter, and health services to meet minimum requirements. The poverty category includes the elderly person living alone who earns $1,000 as well as the family of seven who subsists on $5,000 a year. An urban family of two adults and two children earning less than $3,553 also is designated as living in poverty. A breakdown in the expenditures of this latter group reveals a daily allowance per person of 70 cents for food and $1.40 for other necessities, rent, transportation, clothing, and medical needs. The 13 percent of the population on the poverty level consists of 25 million persons, statistically listed in 10.2 million poor households of families and unrelated individuals.

There are many reasons for poverty: Low levels of ability and limited opportunities for education and training make for low earning capacities, as we noted. Discrimination in all its ugly manifestations hits hardest when it deprives Negroes and other minorities of a wide opportunity to improve their earnings. The aged, the unemployed, and the marginal farmers, together with individuals in broken homes, are additional candidates for poverty rolls.

Since poverty breeds poverty, in outlook and opportunity, it becomes necessary to substitute a pattern of hope in order to put the poor on the road toward full participation in the nation's economic life. Aside from questions of morality and justice, the nation, too, it must be added, benefits in utilizing all its human resources and by creating more customers for its economy.

A recent intensive study of 10 urban ghettos by the United States Department of Labor documented some of the tremendous problems involved in overcoming poverty. The report found that "unemployment in the city slums is so much worse than it is in the country as a whole that the national measurements of unemployment are utterly irrelevant." The study revealed that the unemployment rate in city slums was almost 10 percent, or about three times the national average. "One out of every three residents in the slum has a serious employment problem," the survey declared. It depicted slum unemployment as "primarily a story of inferior education, no skills, police and garnishment records [salary attached for failure to pay bills] discrimination, fatherless children, unnecessarily rigid hiring restrictions and hopelessness."

We have used the term "poverty" up to this point without really attempting to define it. Despite its widespread use today, the term remains a difficult one to nail down. We cannot positively state which family is or is not poor. Any analysis of poverty includes a variety of considerations: family size and age, the level of consumer prices, free lunch and food stamp programs, the use of home-grown food, property owned. Obviously current definitions of poverty would vary considerably from that of yesteryear. Four out of five income earners work for others for a living, whereas in the early years of our country's history income earners were mainly independent farmers. Remember, too, that by American income standards 75 percent of all families in England might be classified as poor.

Attempting to Reduce Poverty

To the President's Council of Economic Advisers, defining poverty in terms of money income seemed the most acceptable way of handling the problem of identification. As we indicated, there is a range (of from $1,000 to $5,000), depending upon the size of the family and other factors.

While the poor have always been with us, they have never been so visible or so vocal. Undoubtedly, the civil rights movement, which highlighted grinding poverty among Negroes, helped to focus on the problem among all groups. Increasingly the poor have been organizing and demonstrating to gain more political powers. Society, thanks to the spotlight cast on the problem by Washington and the nation's press, is sympathetic to what President Johnson called the "War on Poverty." In attempting to break the cycle of deprivation and dependency, the aim is not only to help improve the economic system by the best use of human resources, but also to diminish "juvenile delinquency, crimes of violence, riots and other disorders, often linked with poverty . . ."

Needless to say, a problem involving almost one-eighth of the population admits of no easy solutions. Indeed, experts stress the need to tackle this problem on a broad-based front. We already have mentioned the fact that continued economic growth means more goods and services and more jobs for all, including the poor. Old age security, unemployment insurance, and Medicare can be further improved to aid those in poverty. Direct-action programs under the federal government need constant review and, where necessary, expansion. These programs, authorized under the Economic Opportunity Act of 1964, consist of: (1) a Job Corps that aims to provide high school dropouts with remedial education and training; (2) a neighborhood Youth Corps that provides varied jobs in public agencies or nonprofit organizations for needy teen-agers; (3) a Community Action Program that gives financial support to local antipoverty agencies "designed to stimulate local initiative and comprehensive planning"; (4) other plans, including ones for aid to needy college students, adult education, small business loans, and work opportunities.

Still other antipoverty legislation includes various area redevelopment acts for the depressed areas of Appalachia and the Ozarks; aid to primary and secondary schools and higher education; and the Demonstration Cities Act, which has as its ambitious goal the rebuilding of the blighted areas in which our urban poor live.

In the thinking stage is the idea of an outright annual subsidy to the poor in the form of a "negative income tax," which would serve to eliminate many present welfare programs. "Taxes" would be paid to the poor, just as their more fortunate brethren now pay their taxes to the Internal Revenue Service. The negative income tax proposal aims to put a floor under family income that would bring all those now classified as poor above the poverty line—$3,553 a year for a family of four. Incentives would be included, permitting individuals to retain half their outside earnings, in order to spur people to take jobs. Those arguing for the plan insist that it would reach all the poor; it would restore their dignity, which present relief systems degrade; and it would cut sharply into the present relief bureaucracy. Objectors cite the huge costs involved; the difficulty of using incentive programs; and what they see as an abhorrent philosophy of pay without work. (This and other proposals to alleviate poverty will be discussed in greater detail in a later chapter.)

Much thought in recent years has gone into these poverty campaigns that concentrate on those who remain on the fringes or are seemingly on the outside of the economy. Forced by their persistent unemployment to be onlookers, the poor see others enjoying abundant prosperity; they hear of the availability of jobs but lack the education, training, skills, and even the initiative to seek out those they can fill. A leading study in this field, *Poverty Amid Affluence*, by Oscar Ornati, concludes: "Present-day affluence makes it possible to do away with poverty. If we do not do so now, there is no way of knowing whether the problem will in the future be equally manageable." While there seems to be a great deal of agreement on the seriousness of the problem, as usual, the "solutions" are highly controversial.

PROFITS AND THE ECONOMY

Going from poverty to profits in a discussion on the distribution of income, to those unversed in economics, may seem like a case of cause and effect. In actuality, profits represent in the free market economy the basic incentive to produce and provide the income to business. This income eventually provides the jobs (with income) that help individuals avoid poverty. Profits thus represent the driving force that moves the economy.

Profits essentially involve addition and subtraction. You add up all income—the returns from sales—of your particular business and then you subtract all the expenses involved in selling the product. These expenses will include rent, mortgages, interest on loans, wages, the replacement of equipment, costs of raw materials, and a return on one's own investment of money and time in the enterprise. Profits, hence, are the rewards to enterprisers who are successful in economic arithmetic, to those who manage to maintain a "plus" after subtracting their total costs from their total revenues.

Profits are generally figured in two ways. One way is as a percentage of sales, so much of each dollar of goods sold becomes profit (or loss). The other method involves the amount of profit as a percentage of value of all the company's property, minus its debts. Thus if a company made a profit of $10,000 on its assets of $100,000, it would have a profit of 10 percent. The same company figuring its profit of $10,000 on a basis of $50,000 in sales would have a profit rate of 20 percent. These illustrations demonstrate that the term "profit" as used by the economist is a difficult one to comprehend, for it also involves controversies as to what are actually costs.

Profits are directly related to changes in consumer tastes, changes in production methods, and indeed all the changes that affect a company's total costs and total sales. Fortunate enterprisers who make the right decisions in these varied circumstances will emerge with a profit. It is this profit that encourages business to take the risks necessary for economic growth. In order to increase this profit an enterpriser will be stimulated to produce more efficiently. He will spend much time planning the kinds of products consumers will want and can afford. He will concentrate on research not only to give him a new or improved product, but also to see that the best techniques of production will be used to keep his costs down and his profits up. He will maintain a permanent appraisal as a part of his effort to get the best possible uses of his trio of scarce items: manpower, machines, and natural resources.

Finally, businessmen are guided by the possibility of high profits into the production of goods and services most desired by consumers. Losses reveal the possibility of too much production or absence of demand. Losses also may reveal that certain producers are inefficient and cannot compete with their more efficient brethren. Businesses reserve a considerable part of their profits in order to expand their production, to modernize or replace worn-out equipment. Desirous of sharing in the profits distributed as dividends, millions of people risk their savings for a chance of future gain by buying stock in companies of their choices. Risk-taking, together with the possibility of profit, thus is a key factor in understanding the distribution of income.

In single ownership and partnership enterprises, profits go to the owners, who may use them for personal buying or for further investment in the business. These profits are then taxed as part of the owner's personal income. Profits in the corporation are channeled in three directions: There is a corporate profits tax that must be paid. A certain percentage is usually retained as undistributed profits for capital expansion and rebuilding. Depending upon the specific decision of the board of directors, some of the profits also are distributed as dividend payments to stockholders.

There is wide disagreement as to how high profits must be to get enterprisers to enter or to stay in business. As a necessary function, however, profits remain at the core of the free market system: Without profits there simply would be no private businesses.

WAGES AND SALARIES

Just as the anticipation of profits activates production (consumption, too) by businessmen, so does the receipt of wages provide income for wage earners to buy the goods and services produced by the businessmen. This income, of course, is an expense to the producer. In fact it is the largest part of his costs. Wages also represent—not surprisingly in view of the 76.6 million people at work—70 percent of the annual functional distribution of income. (See "National Income" table.) Profits and wages, like rival suitors, constantly vie with each other for the gains of productivity: the outpouring of more goods and services for greater earnings.

Dividing National Income, 1968
(in billions)

Wages and Salaries	$ 514
Unincorporated Businesses (farmers, single ownerships, partners, independent professionals: doctors, lawyers)	63
Profits Earned by Corporations	89
Income from Rents	21
Income from Interest	26
Total National Income	$ 713

SOURCE: Economic Report of the President, January 1969 (figures rounded).

Again, just as the more efficient producer who meets the demands of consumers is in a position to make more profits, so is he therefore prepared to pay better wages. Better wages reflect the demand and supply for each type of labor in each special market. Naturally, labor prefers higher wages to lower ones. Thus labor will move to higher-paying industries because producers compete among themselves to supply goods and services to areas of increasing consumer demand. A janitor working in a hotel can expect less pay than one in a steel company, since steel industries generally pay higher wages for all jobs on an industry-wide basis than do service industries. By learning the skills of a different occupation, say a lathe operator, the janitor can, of course, increase his income still more.

Producers taking on additional help must consider what the extra worker would contribute to production and what he would cost. If wages are high, the producer may seek to limit his labor needs by improving the technical requirements of production with more effective tools and equipment. Of course the businessman can absorb additional wage costs by raising the prices of his goods. His competitors, however, with different ideas about the market for higher-priced goods may not permit this escape route. Remember that business competes for labor, but also competes to keep costs down for greater profits.

Productivity, the amount of goods and services each worker produces per man-hour, determines the "top" as well as the "bottom" wage that the businessman will pay. As the minimum rate for elevator operators (unskilled labor) in large cities rose to about $2.50 an hour, owners in metropolitan areas invested in automated elevators. At this wage rate, considered by owners to be above the productivity of these unskilled workers, the investment required to automate elevators was quickly returned. Within a few years elevator buttons became more common than elevator men.

Minimum wage rates (now $1.60 an hour) under the Fair Labor Standards Act also tend to reduce employment for those with the least training and experience. Even these low wages cannot in some cases be justified by their low productivity. In these cases, where workers do not produce enough to earn a minimum rate of $1.60 an hour, employers hire fewer of these marginal or below-level workers. Those unfortunates who thus do not meet productivity standards either drift into industries with lower wage scales not covered by minimum wage standards or join the ranks of the unemployed. It seems clear, therefore, that minimum wage legislation does not benefit all workers. Most individuals probably would benefit more by having their level of education and skills raised or by having society subsidize their family incomes.

Up to this point we have concentrated on the demand for labor. There is another cutting edge to our market scissors which we must, of course, consider: The *specific* supply of labor for *specific* markets. (Keep in mind the fact that human beings, unlike impersonal raw materials, have some say in how they shall be treated in the market.) They may refuse for many reasons to move to other areas where better jobs await, or they may be ignorant of job opportunities. You will note that we emphasize the specific nature of both demand and supply of labor. This simply emphasizes the fact that specialized industries such as textiles, steel, aerospace call for varieties of education, training, and skill. Wage rates also will depend upon the supply of skilled, semiskilled, and unskilled workers needed. Skilled architects, engineers, and physicists, because of specialized abilities and lengthy training, as we noted, will naturally be in a scarcer category than semiskilled mechanics whose training may require less than a year, or unskilled assembly line workers for whom a month's briefing is adequate.

To repeat: Differences in wage rates come about because enterprising businessmen seek special types of labor to produce efficiently goods and services that consumers desire. Competing with other businessmen for this labor, they help to bid up prices (wages). The amount of specialized labor seeking these jobs will help to determine the specific wage rates. Higher wages will attract labor resources to where the action is: that is, to industries that produce goods that consumers want. Changes in wage rates will occur when conditions affecting the demand or supply of labor change.

INCOME AND THE ECONOMY

Consumer buying patterns are always changing. Tomorrow, sweeping changes may occur in the nation's entertainment habits through the speedy advent of subscription television. Today, the use of a synthetic shoe material like Corfam challenges the traditional role of leather. Consumers are spending more on such items as education and insurance and less on apparel and food. Manufacturing, partly as a result, is decreasing proportionately as service industries are increasing. Labor, responding to these changes, is attracted to industries on the upgrade and away from those sliding away from consumer demand. Farm employment, declining by approximately 400,000 or 7 percent in 1966, illustrates an industry's downward trend. Mainly because of the low returns earned by agricultural labor, compared with better wages available in nonfarm jobs, there is a tremendous inducement to leave the farm for the city. This movement, however, also serves as a more efficient distribution of the nation's labor force by attracting labor to industries where the greatest consumer demands exist.

Wage levels also are affected by the cost of living and unemployment in different sections of the country. Obviously, a lower cost of living increases *real wages* by raising the purchasing power of each dollar earned. Thus a lower wage in one area may be comparable to a higher wage in a different area. If one section has a higher unemployment rate on the average than others, employers may be encouraged to lower their wage offers.

THE AMERICAN LABOR FORCE

While wage rates are determined by the demand for specific types of labor for specific industries, they also must be considered in terms of the total labor supply available. In 1968 this *labor force,* the number of civilians over 16 years of age who work, or are willing to work, for 15 hours or more per week, numbered more than 82 million in a population of over 200 million. The bulk of the 40 percent of the population who labor is composed of workers 20 to 60 years of age. Compulsory school attendance and child labor laws, together with better provision for old age security, have squeezed both ends out of the labor force.

Other characteristics of the continuously changing American labor force include: (1) *Mobility*. Millions each year move within their states or to other states in search of better job opportunities. (2) *Education.* The average education attainment of new workers keeps increasing. The high school graduate is well represented in the ranks of the employed. Formal education is continually supplemented by industrial training courses and adult education courses under union and school supervision. (3) *Composition.* For the last 10 years the number of white collar jobs (clerical, professional, and technical) has exceeded the number of blue collar (factory) ones. Service positions now outnumber those on production lines. Continuing changes along these lines are projected in the accompanying table. (4) *Women.* The proportion of women is now one-third of the labor force. Increasingly, married women with older children seek jobs. This trend is expected to raise the percentage of women in the labor force.

Mere numbers will not give you the full story of the labor force, although the proportion of the population involved and the average number of hours worked per week (now 40) are obviously important. (An increase or decrease of hours worked gives us a vital multiplier for the total number of man-hours available, thus in effect increasing or decreasing the labor force.) But it is labor's qualities—its adaptability, its intelligence, its skill, education, and ability—that determine the *actual* value of the numbers in the labor force. These qualities account for the superiority of the American labor force to the superior numbers of, for instance, the Indian and Chinese labor forces.

THE CHANGING LABOR FORCE

Distribution of the Labor Force by Age Group and Sex, 1965 and 1975 (in millions)

	1965		1975	
Age	Male	Female	Male	Female
16–19	3.8	2.5	4.7	3.2
20–34	16.8	7.7	23.3	11.0
35–54	21.6	11.4	21.5	12.6
55+	8.9	4.6	9.9	6.0

Percent Racial Distribution, Occupational Groups

Occupation	Nonwhite Employed 1964	Nonwhite Employed 1967	White Employed 1967
Professional Tech.	6.7	7.3	14.0
Farmer, Farm Mgr.	1.9	1.3	2.8
Managers, Proprietor	2.6	2.6	11.0
Clerical	7.6	11.2	17.2
Sales	1.8	1.8	6.6
Craftsmen	7.0	7.6	13.9
Operatives	20.3	23.5	18.1
Private Household	13.6	10.4	1.4
Service Workers	18.7	19.1	9.1
Farm Laborers	6.8	4.0	1.9
Laborers (Nonfarm)	13.0	11.3	4.0

Jobs and Youth 16–21 Years of Age, 1967

	White		Negro	
	In School	Out of School	In School	Out of School
Labor Force	2,518,000	6,414,000	243,000	987,000
Employed	2,264,000	5,822,000	176,000	783,000
Unemployed	254,000	592,000	68,000	203,000
JOBLESS RATE	10.1%	9.2%	27.7%	20.8%
Not in Labor Force[a]	5,200,000	2,488,000	812,000	447,000
Male	2,522,000	479,000	393,000	88,000
Female	2,678,000	2,008,000	419,000	360,000

[a]Not working and not actively seeking work.
SOURCE FOR ALL THREE TABLES: U.S. Bureau of Labor Statistics.

Unions and Income Distribution

Returning to labor's supply in particular markets for teachers, plumbers, librarians, scientists, and technicians—where wage rates are set—we discover situations that hinder the operation of demand and supply in these markets. People being what they are, personal motives and preferences appear in their attitudes toward the job market, much as they do in other situations. Again, ignorance of better job opportunities is a frequent barrier to matching demand and the supply of labor. Workers frequently refuse to pull up roots in one community no matter how attractive career situations are in another area. Labor unions, for collective reasons, also exercise control over the demand and supply of labor in particular markets.

Just as employers try to get labor services at the lowest prices, workers, with the aid of labor unions, try to command the highest prices for their labor. By *collective bargaining* (the union acts for all workers that it represents, instead of having each worker bargain individually) workers increase their power by controlling—or cutting off—the supply of labor in a specific industry. This permits them to press harder for higher wages and better working conditions. Unions reinforce labor's claim that it contributes to increased productivity and therefore should have its just share of this increase. Unfortunately, there are also other claimants, management and stockholders, who argue for their split in a situation where there are few objective answers.

About one-fourth of the labor force (18 out of 82 million) are union members. Proportionately more (one-half) of the labor force in manufacturing, a traditional union stronghold, are unionized. Continued growth of the white collar segment of the labor force, a fact we noted earlier, has caused the rate of union membership to slow down: white collar workers, for many reasons, are more difficult to organize, but this situation is changing.

In industries where unions are strong, such as steel, automobiles, and rubber, unions can exert strong pressures over a short period of time to push wages up. Even here, however, unions have not eliminated supply and demand. Employers must still consider consumer demand and the price for products that labor helps to produce. Productivity, in areas of greatest union activity, as elsewhere, ultimately will determine what employers can pay. If increased labor costs cannot be made up by cutting down on other production costs through more efficient management, improved techniques, or new technology, then the price of the manufacturer's product must be raised. If consumers refuse to buy the product at the higher price there will be obvious cutbacks in production—and job losses. Then again, if wage increases are widespread throughout all industries, prices in general may rise. The ensuing inflation also increases labor's cost of living, thus robbing them of union-won gains. Interestingly enough, labor's share of the national income has not changed much in the last 60 years: about 70 percent of the national income continues to go to wage earners.

Labor unions also bargain for *fringe benefits*. These are extra benefits such as pensions, insurance, paid vacations and holidays, and supplementary unemployment insurance benefits, in addition to regular wages. The important point to remember here is that while these items may not immediately be received as cash by workers, they are expenses to the employer and are so considered by him when he adds up his bill for labor. Again, consumer demand and productivity must be considered.

Distribution of income, whether it refers to wages, salaries, rent, dividends, or profit, ultimately comes from involvement in production. Despite some strong obstacles set up by capital and labor, the market forces of supply and demand remain powerful magnets for drawing the highest incomes to those whose particular services are in greatest demand. Only by increasing total income by economic growth, however, can we basically satisfy the desire of different sectors of the economy for increased income.

CHAPTER 5

THE CHALLENGE OF STABILIZING THE ECONOMY

Leveling the "Ups and Downs"

It is not enough to have the economy respond in satisfactory fashion to the three leading economic questions: What will be produced and how much? How will it be produced? And for whom will it be produced? In addition to answering these questions, an economy must meet the challenge of keeping the employment of people and the prices of goods at a fairly even level (*economic stability*).

In order to maintain stability the economy must avoid *inflation* (a sharp increase in the general level of prices) and *recession* (a falling off in business). Inflation inflicts cruel burdens on many sections of the economy as dollars lose their value. Recession is an equally serious problem with its waste of resources, and with men and machines idle because of bad business conditions.

No economic system is either perfect or static. The price-directed market system, in attempting somehow to account for the tastes and preferences of all people, is uniquely dynamic. Millions of decisions, many of them depending upon the unpredictable future, involve numerous risks to producers and consumers alike. New products like synthetic fibers jostle the cotton, wool, and silk markets. Businesses fail for valid as well as foolish reasons. Jobs are lost or disappear because of changing technology. Consumers, despite attempts by surveys to foretell future actions, remain unpredictable in their preferences. For that matter, accurately predicting what businessmen will do also is risky. To cite but one example: A giant cereal company recently built a multimillion-dollar plant to produce cereal with freeze-dried strawberries, peaches, and blueberries. Despite a relatively high price, initial sales were good —but few customers came back for more. In an effort to recoup its losses the company sponsored research in additives to foods that it hopes will reduce dental decay. But again, even if this research is successful, there is no guarantee that the new products will sell.

We all are interested in seeing that our nation's economic power is used steadily and fully, as well as efficiently, by putting resources to their best use. We desire this economic stability while developing new methods and new products to maintain consumer preference.

Keeping the economy balanced at the same time that it makes progress at a proper rate of economic growth means, to state it negatively, that it avoids inflation or recession.

Just as thermometers, blood counts, and cardiograms give doctors indications of a patient's changing condition, so has economics developed *indicators*, or statistical signals, that reveal to those with knowledge the direction in which the economy is going. And, just as doctors learn that some readings are more significant than others, so economists stress the interpretation of some statistics more than others in predicting the direction or trend of economic developments. Thus out of the eighty-odd indicators of varied economic activities, the economist may settle for quick readings of a baker's dozen. We will discuss some of the better-known measuring devices that serve to give us some rough ideas where we are going on our economic road.

MEASURING ECONOMIC ACTIVITY

Perhaps the best-known index of economic activity is the *Gross National Product* (GNP), which is the estimated final dollar value of all the goods and services produced in the United States in any one year. In an economy such as ours, the GNP includes a fantastic variety of goods, from combs to airplanes, and of services, from haircuts to surgery. The common denominator that permits all these diverse goods and services to be totaled are their price tags—the money value set by the market. The GNP measures total spending; it indicates changes in the amount of present business activity as compared with other economic periods; and it shows (as the next chapter will describe in greater detail) how living standards change from time to time.

Three measures of income are related to the concept of the GNP. These so-called "cousins" are National Income (NI), Personal Income (PI), and Disposable Income (DI). *National Income* represents the total income received by those contributing to current production: labor, natural resources, capital, and entrepreneurs. NI covers wages, profits, dividends, as well as interest and rents. *Personal Income* measures income received by individuals or households, but does not include income received by corporations. Money paid to the government for Social Security or unemployment insurance is not included, but benefits from these and other government payments are. *Disposable Income* is what remains after one pays his taxes. The "remainder" can either be spent or saved. Disposable income gives us a pretty good idea of the actual amount of purchasing power in the hands of consumers—certainly a vital statistic, even if it does not tell us what he will do with it, or where he can get more (savings or loans).

We also should be familiar with *index numbers.* These statistical devices help us to compare the rate of industrial production or the cost of living for different periods of time. A *Consumer Price Index* (CPI), for example, is issued monthly by the Federal Bureau of Labor Statistics. This is based on the market price of items a typical family might buy. The prices are averaged and compared with those of the years 1957–1959, which is regarded as a base or average period. Since the base period is given the number 100, any variation in average prices will show whether living costs are going up or down. In 1969 the CPI was 128.2. This means that consumer prices on the average were 28.2 percent more than those in the base year. Glancing back farther to 1961 on our graph will show the price climb in recent years.

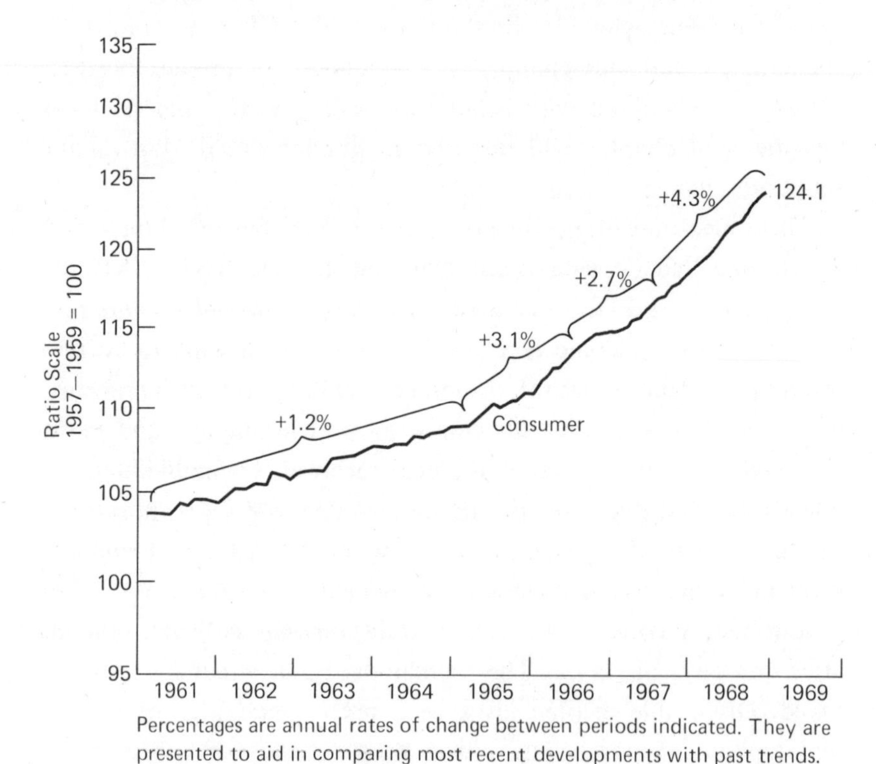

Fig. 6. Prices. (See appendix table 3.)

There are many other measurements, such as those of wages and salaries, industrial production, corporate profits, freight car loadings, and the unemployment rate, which help to give the economist information as to the general health of the economy. Diagnosing the ills of the nation's economy, as in the case of an individual, is tricky business. Indeed, the economist's technical equipment needs considerable improvement before it can compare with that of the physician! Yet we need economic diagnosis, in order to provide "remedies" for the ills of recession and inflation; and we need accurate forecasting to help avoid future troubles. Increasingly, however, the problems of the economist become more difficult as a result of the unbelievable complexity of modern economic life. Thousands upon thousands of industries depend upon thousands of other industries for raw materials, tools, communications, transportation, funds, and customers. All sections of the country are interrelated and, in addition, there is a significant dependence on international markets. Above all, the market economy sanctions millions of independent decisions, which, when totalled, affect the direction and vitality of the economy.

The use of estimates of national income accounting—the GNP and its cousins— started less than 40 years ago. They provide useful tools for determining national economic policy, tools that past generations lacked. They also have helped to educate the nation to overcome previous attitudes of *laissez-faire* (let alone) toward the economy; this attitude was to let the economy cure itself without government interference. So far have we departed from this view that Congress, with the support of both Republicans and Democrats, passed the Employment Act of 1946, which pledges the federal government to promote "maximum employment, production and purchasing power." Exactly how this should be done, when, and to what extent are, as one would expect, matters of strong disagreement among economists. Few economists, however, argue against the principle of government action to prevent recession or inflation through its ability to raise or lower taxes, or to control the amount of money and credit in circulation.

INSTABILITY AND ITS CAUSES

A *recession* can be recognized by a drop in the GNP and national income, accompanied by growing unemployment, falling production of goods and services, and declining profits. When a recession lasts for some time and its effects are widespread, then it is referred to as a depression. Thus the Great Depression of the 1930s, which lasted 10 years, was marked by nearly 13 million unemployed, or one-fourth of the labor force. In human terms these were days—and years—of great emptiness and deprivation. Skipped paychecks flattened wallets and punctured bank accounts, giving rise to hungry and frustrated households. For the economy, the depression also reflected aspects of a wasteland, with huge gaps in the statistical record for the production of goods and services that never took place. It has been estimated (in terms of 1956 dollars) that the unemployed facilities of the 1930s could have produced an additional $650 billion in goods and services—a permanent loss to the economy.

Four recessions since World War II (1949, 1953, 1957, and 1960) each lasted a year or less, but their total effects were mild by comparison with the depression of the 1930s. Fortunately, the economic community learned a great deal from that depression so that today the chances are extremely slim that a recession could develop into a depression.

Inflation is marked by a noticeable rise in the general level of prices as indicated by the Consumer Price Index. In an inflationary period, goods will cost more today than the same goods cost awhile back, and they will cost even more in the days to come. More dollars will now be required to purchase an equivalent amount of goods. If prices inch up the CPI scale at a relatively slow but steady pace, this increase is usually referred to as creeping inflation. If the pace remains one of slow price increases, harmful effects are not immediately apparent to many in the economy.

However, people living on fixed incomes, such as those dependent on pensions or savings, are particularly hurt by a reduction in the purchasing power of their dollars. Since they are in no position to bargain for an increased amount of dollars, this group faces a situation where the dollars they regularly receive go down in purchasing value over a period of inflationary time. For the past 10 years the value of the dollar in terms of purchasing power has dropped to where it now buys, on the average, 72 cents worth of goods and services.

When prices rise at a furious pace we have a situation known as galloping inflation. Uruguay, for instance, underwent a price rise in 1967 that sent the cost of living skyrocketing by 136 percent. So marked was the inflationary gallop that price tags disappeared from almost all goods because shopkeepers found it tiresome to keep changing the tags daily as prices leaped upward.

In the United States since World War II there have been four creeping inflationary periods: 1946–1948, 1950–1952, 1957–1958, and more recently a strong upward spiral that started in 1965, with the enormously increased spending for the Vietnam War.

Instability in the economy—recession and inflation—can be traced to changes in total spending of consumers, government, and businessmen. If this spending falls off to any great degree, goods do not get sold, profits decline, and businessmen are forced to cut back production. As a result, unemployment mounts and therefore people buy even less, and businessmen further reduce their production.

Under conditions where productive resources (labor, capital, and raw materials) are being fully used, total spending will cause prices to rise if demand is greater than the amount of goods and services available. This action of "too many dollars chasing too few goods" spells inflation.

Consumer moods vary as they interpret the many signals about economic activity. Will wages rise? Will prices fall? Will inflation continue, or possibly increase? Will the economy decline? Eventually these moods influence economic actions. Fortunately, we have a concrete example to illustrate consumer reactions. The Survey Research Center of the University of Michigan reported that in February 1967 consumer sentiment for purchasing homes, cars, appliances, and other consumer goods turned upward after 14 months of decline. In attempting to find out what developments had created "doubt and uncertainty for over a year," the Center discovered the following reasons: Consumers resented "sizable price increases" and postponed some purchases; rising interest rates handicapped business activity; an expected rise in income taxes reduced purchasing power; and the Vietnam war's influence on the domestic economy was interpreted as leading to inflation and higher taxes. Toward the end of the 14-month period no new unfavorable developments appeared, and people learned to live with the existing unfavorable ones. Interest rates dropped, as did the rate of price increases. These developments, added to the fact that many families enjoyed frequent and substantial increases in income, caused consumers to become more optimistic about purchasing goods. Thus this survey illustrates in some detail the importance—and the uncertainties—of consumer spending to the stability of the economy.

Curiously enough, however, consumer spending of late has been extremely stable. About 93 percent of consumer income is spent every year. How much is spent, of course, will depend upon how much is earned. If unemployment is widespread, it stands to reason that Personal Income will be less, and therefore the total amount available for spending will have to be less. Or if taxes are sharply increased, the Disposable Personal Income is decreased and a similar situation results. On the other hand, of course, increased income—unless inflation cuts into the dollar's value—will boost the amount available for consumer purchasing.

Exactly how consumer income will be spent (color TV or a new automobile, new clothes or travel) is something businessmen would love to know in advance, but are denied the opportunity. Prosperity may be present, but not all businessmen share equally in its gifts. Consumers may be well stocked with television sets, refrigerators, automobiles, or other durable items. When they *trim* these purchases, they affect a host of other industries that supply parts and raw materials to manufacturers of durables. Consumer tastes, as we have repeatedly indicated, are hard to predict and even fickle. Clothing manufacturers who depend upon changes in style for much of their business would willingly attest to this judgment.

Government spending, which accounts for one-fifth of the GNP, is obviously an important part of total spending. Unlike consumers or businessmen, government spending is not so dependent on present income. Government, of course, can borrow more freely than either group and can more easily plan for long-range projects. Government spending also can be used for a greater variety of purchases than either group could possibly dream of, from safety pins to spaceships. Government spending, for whatever purpose, contributes toward maintaining or increasing total spending, income, and employment. A reduction in this spending serves to decrease income and employment.

An increase in taxation, by reducing the income of consumers and businessmen, takes money out of circulation and results in less private spending—especially if taxes are greater than government spending. A tax cut, as in 1964, permitted consumers and businessmen to spend more, since they now had more income left. When government spending is greater than its tax income, there is even more money left for total spending, since more is being pumped into the economy while less is being taken out.

Thus taxing and spending are tools that the government can use to help maintain the stability of the economy. Changes in the size of federal tax collections, their timing, and the kinds of taxes are watched by economists for their influence on the economy. Even the public has come to realize that there is a basic difference in the purpose of the government budget as compared with the family budget. In periods of slack activity with accompanying high unemployment and factories working at less than capacity, unbalanced budgets may serve a useful purpose by stimulating production and employment. This was dramatized in 1964 when the tax cut was passed in order to increase purchasing power. At the time, the budget was unbalanced, and there was a growing government need for funds to continue government spending. This spending, plus the additional money available from the tax cut, served as a sort of double shot-in-the-arm for the economy. Some claim that this tax cut helped to reduce unemployment from a rate of 5.4 percent to 3.7 percent!

There are also built-in automatic stabilizers that help to soften recessions. In all four postwar recessions, government expenditures for unemployment insurance rose while income tax collections dropped, reflecting the decline in individual incomes. Jointly, these automatic devices were extremely helpful in maintaining purchasing power.

Unfortunately, not all governmental decisions follow the dictates of economic logic. Politics sometimes blurs the vision of administration officials in recognizing (at least publicly) that signs of recession are setting in, and then further incapacitates them in acting on these signals. Then, too, certain government programs for which long-time plans have been made are often not changed, although changing economic conditions may call for change. Political realities being what they are, it is, of course, easier to get a tax cut from Congress rather than a needed tax increase—especially in an election year.

Consumer and government spending have proved more predictable than private investment (business spending on tools, equipment, new factories, and goods). As business purchases increase or decrease, they cause the economy to expand and contract. How does one account for the frequent swings in business investment? Perhaps the basic reason is that the businessman in seeking profits must estimate the future. Depending upon whether his view is optimistic or pessimistic, investments will rise or fall. This optimism or pessimism, of course, will depend upon changing economic situations and how businessmen interpret these changes. In turn, what businessmen actually do will affect the state of the economy. Thus after a long period of prosperity industry may have increased its investment to the point where it has more than enough capacity to produce for current demand. Businessmen will now cut back their investment orders until such time as capital equipment needs replacement, or increased consumer demand requires further expansion. These cutbacks will result in less business for the suppliers of capital equipment, who also will be forced to reduce their production and discharge their workers. Thus cutbacks in investments have a chain reaction type of effect upon the economy.

Similarly, business spending on goods stocked for future sales (*inventories*) will fall off if the market is saturated and the businessman's signals turn pessimistic. Optimistic flashes will occur when the inventories get used up and reorders become necessary because of increased demand. And, as we noted in our discussion of productivity (Chapter 2), the development of new products and important changes in technology can cause changes in investment spending. Here the new items or new ways of doing things usually benefit from torrents of funds spent for new investments, while the older competing products or older methods of production may be forced to subsist on trickling (or even dried up) funds.

At any rate, these fluctuations in business spending affect consumer income, which itself derives from the volume of business activity. As consumer incomes fall, spending also may decrease. Hence business is further affected in its downward descent and profits tumble further. This action reinforces the relationship we have continually indicated in examples of the circular flow of income: Changes in production will affect incomes, and hence consumer spending, which in turn will affect business income, and so on.

THE CYCLES OF BUSINESS

There have been 31 business recessions of varying intensity and duration in the United States since 1834. Economists distinguish four phases in business cycles, of which recession represents one phase, and depression, recovery, and prosperity the other three.

Recession

A *recession* marks a downturn in business with declines in production, incomes, and employment. It may start with a decline in business investment, which, as we have seen, soon causes a drop in employment, in income, and in consumer purchases. These actions interact upon each other, causing a "snowballing" effect. Checking the economic indicators at this stage we discover that they abound with depressing readings. The GNP, statistics related to income, and those concerned with unemployment, industrial production, and other important areas register sharp declines. With each decline there is a falling off in the optimistic spirit of businessmen. Recessions, unlike depressions, are relatively mild affairs, both in their shorter span of time and the fewer number of industries and individuals affected.

Depression

When the recession continues to be weighted with falling indicators, over a long period of time it hits an economic bottom, which is called a *depression*. Unemployment, declining business investment, and a drop in consumer spending further jostle each other into positions at the bottom of the particular trough into which the economy has fallen. A depression marks a serious low point in all the key indicators of an economy's health and is further characterized by the lengthy period of illness, which affects production, employment, and incomes. The depression of the

1930s, to which we alluded earlier, lasted for more than a decade and caused many thousands of businesses to go bankrupt and many millions of people to be unemployed.

Recovery

Recovery is connected with increases in demand. To keep going, businessmen and consumers must continue certain basic spending, even at the expense of their savings. Both groups also must replace worn-out items and equipment. Unemployment insurance and other benefits—the automatic built-in stabilizers mentioned earlier—come to the rescue and provide additional needed income for consumer purchases. Government, with various relief and work projects, also will supply needed transfusions of money to aid the economy's recovery.

Prosperity

Prosperity, the peak of the economic cycle, is decorated with bright economic indicators flashing their encouraging signals. Of course, an extended period of prosperity will change the intensity of some of these indicators. Overinvestment or overextended inventories may now generate cloudy signals, pointing to a possible recession. Or signs may now be pointing toward inflation.

Thus, after five years of unprecedented peacetime growth uninterrupted by recession or marred by inflation, the United States economy faced a new test: holding down inflationary pressures generated by increased spending begun in mid-1965 as a result of the Vietnam war. Wholesale prices, after holding almost perfectly stable for seven years, started to rise in 1965. In the fall of 1966 housewives, aroused by rising consumer prices (3 percent) picketed food stores all across the country. The dramatic action of the housewives seemed to highlight the nation's concern about rising prices (and their consequences), which became an issue in the elections of that year.

INFLATION AND ITS DANGERS

Inflation is a major illness, along with recessions and depressions, of a stable economy. It is related to the business cycle in that a sudden reversal of inflation usually brings with it a drop in overall business. Generally, the higher the inflation, the greater the ensuing decline.

Inflation, a noticeable increase in the level of prices caused by an excess of total demand for foods and services, can best be charted by following the Consumer Price Index and the declining purchasing power of the dollar. We can determine by following this indicator if price increases are general, and then see if they are following a continuing pattern. Again, inflation occurs when consumer, business, and government spending increase faster than the economy's capacity to produce. Total demand will then exceed the total amount that can be supplied and prices will rise. How fast they will rise depends upon the pressures of demand and the limitations of supply.

Unchecked, or galloping inflation, is usually accompanied by the government's printing of money at a furious rate, in a mistaken attempt to keep up with rising prices. The classic case in modern times occurred in Germany, where wholesale prices rose more than a trillion times from 1920 to 1923. German mortgages, worth 10 billion dollars in 1913, 10 years later could have been paid off with one United States penny! More recently, Brazil underwent a somewhat similar experience. From 1942–1962 the cost of living went up 3000 percent. While still not under control in 1966 (when the cost of living increased by 41 percent) that year was a marked improvement over 1964, with its increase of 84 percent! Even more recently, Uruguay's peso within a period of 20 months dropped from 100 to 300 to the dollar. In human terms, a government employee described the effects of galloping inflation: "It is as if we all had to take a huge pay cut. We can't afford to paint our houses, buy cars, or take vacations. For most of us, it means having to work at two or three jobs just to keep going."

While the United States, fortunately, cannot match the German and Brazilian experiences, it has, nevertheless, undergone a number of serious inflations. All major inflations in this country have occurred as a result of wars: the War of 1812, the Civil War, World Wars I and II, and the Korean and Vietnam wars. During a war, jobs at good salaries are usually available. Civilian goods, however, are generally scarce because of the necessity to produce war supplies. Money saved awaits the return (after the war) of increased civilian goods, but there is an interval where demand, backed by readily available cash, swamps the limited supply of goods and services.

Milder, or creeping inflation, also occurs during any era when the economy operates at full employment and demand exceeds supply. There are also situations where certain industries practicing monopolistic types of control over prices can force up their own prices, an increase which may be accompanied by wage increases. In turn, these price increases may force other industries to raise their prices. When costs push up prices, the resulting inflation is called *cost push*. If purchasers pull up prices by demand, the inflation is referred to as *demand-pull*.

We are more readily aware of the obvious evils of recession and depression than we are of the dangers of inflation. When men and machines are idle on a large scale, aside from the visible economic waste for society, there also are countless obvious personal frustrations and tragedies. Inflation, especially in its earlier stages, indicates fewer dangers to the economy. Indeed, rising prices and rising wages may actually be attractive to considerable sectors of the population. Speculators in stocks and real estate may welcome the higher prices attached to their holdings and may look forward to increased profits. Businessmen sell goods on hand for higher prices before rising costs cut into their profits. Labor relishes the idea of taking home extra dollars.

Inflation, however, soon exacts its own price for the temporary advantages. For as prices rise on raw materials and labor, and as the cost of borrowing money goes up, a squeeze on profits sets in. Workers also find that the cost of living cuts down the advantages of the extra dollars they receive. If we project the 3 percent annual increase in prices of the past few years, we find that prices will double in 22 years.

The basic attitude toward inflation has been compared to a fat lady eating candy. No one can really guarantee her that by sacrificing sweets she will immediately gain a svelte figure. Nor can she be told that great harm will befall her by eating another piece of that candy from which she receives so much satisfaction. But it stands to reason that continued overindulgence will become hazardous. So is it with economic overindulgence, which leads to inflation.

According to Arthur M. Okun, former Chairman of the Council on Economic Advisers, whose analogy this is, "There is a natural and understandable resistance to the timely adoption of anti-inflationary policies when the economy advances too rapidly." The policies that work against inflation, however, "are essentially unpleasant medicines." Tax increases are immediately felt, but their benefits in curbing price increases are less apparent. Reducing government expenditures means sacrificing programs that benefit the nation. And raising the cost or the availability of credit means that loans for housing and municipal governments become more difficult.

Severe periods of inflation ultimately disrupt the economy, are unfair to many groups, and may lead to financial collapse. The cheapened dollar makes it difficult for business to make decisions connected with goods already on hand and to figure the depreciation of buildings and machines. Inflation also "robs the market baskets" of those who live on fixed incomes: pensions, insurance proceeds, savings accounts, and bonds. These investments have a stated value, and rising prices mean that the dollars a person gets back have less buying power than those he originally put in. Wage increases tend to lag behind price increases in such job categories as teaching, government, and the service industries. When food prices are affected, as often happens, low-income families are hit disproportionately hard. President Johnson bluntly labeled inflation "a pickpocket." Poverty-ridden families, reflecting on the 10 percent rise in food prices from 1964–1968, would quickly echo his views! Inflationary pressures that cheapen the value of the dollar also weaken international confidence in the dollar, which has become the leading international currency. Foreign holders of dollars—some $30 billion—use them as the main vehicle for international transactions. As we will see in a later chapter, an erosion of confidence in the dollar can vitally affect international markets and our own balance-of-payments problem. Higher prices for American goods also make it more difficult to sell them abroad. Finally, when inflation gets out of hand, as we observed in the cases of Germany and Brazil, financial collapse is the penalty the economy must pay.

Treating Instability: Fiscal Policy

There are no formulas or ready-made answers to the problem of instability. Few economists today would argue for letting the "natural" law of supply and demand take its course as a cure for the ills of instability. Economists, like medical doctors, disagree among themselves about what precise steps should be taken, their priority and timing. Since money is to business what blood is to the human system, economic doctors concentrate on regulating the disorders of instability through the main arteries of the economy. This is mainly accomplished by using fiscal policy and monetary policy, depending upon the need, to speed up or to slow down effective demand for goods and services.

When we resort to *fiscal policy* to fight inflation or recession, we are using the taxing and spending power of the federal government. Recall that government purchases of goods and services now amount to about 20 percent of GNP. Through its purchases of goods and services, or its transfer payments to veterans, old age and insurance benefits, interest on bonds, and farm subsidies, the government helps to maintain or increase total spending during a period of recession. By increasing spending it increases income and employment, which, of course, are interrelated. On the other hand, inflation would call for a possible reduction in government spending, in order to help "cool" the fevered spending of the rest of the economy by not bidding for goods already in short supply.

Another aspect of fiscal policy involves taxation. Increasing taxes reduces the amount of money available to consumers and business, thus reducing excessive private spending. If this action of increasing taxes is coupled with a decrease in public spending, it will have the effect of creating a *surplus* (tax income exceeds spending) thus reducing total spending. Such action would be favored during an inflationary period.

A *budget deficit* (spending exceeds tax income) would be prescribed for a recession. This would involve decreased taxation, together with increased spending, thus adding to total spending. The *national debt* (what the federal government owes) will increase when there is a budget deficit because the federal government will be forced to borrow money by selling government bonds. Since the government will have to pay interest on this money, the borrowing when properly managed further serves to add to purchasing power.

Fiscal policy is a powerful medicine for helping an ailing (and a healthy) economy. Changes in federal spending and tax policies quickly and directly affect the disposable income of consumers and businessmen. Since both taxing and spending are accomplished through the political process (Congress and the President) it is sometimes difficult to get speedy or unpopular action, especially for tax increases. Moreover, spending programs are involved and the time interval often may be too long to be effective. Government spending calls for legislative authorization of projects, subsequent allocation of moneys, and competitive bidding by private interests. By the time this intricate process is completed, the conditions that originally called for more spending may have changed considerably.

Treating Instability: Monetary Policy

Monetary policy, which supplements fiscal policy, calls for regulating the amount of money and credit in the economy. The Federal Reserve System, which consists of a Federal Reserve Bank in Washington and 12 major regional banks, is empowered by Congress to regulate bank lending.

By far the most important money used is in the form of checking accounts. Another name for this money is *demand deposits,* or checkbook money, which can be obtained "on demand" from commerical banks. Well over 90 percent of business transactions are conducted through these paper orders to banks to pay others from existing checking accounts. Checkbook money accounts for $140 billion of the total United States money supply of $180 billion. These accounts are built up from deposits as well as by loans from banks. When consumers, business, or the government borrow (or deposit money) from commercial banks, a demand deposit or checking account money is created at the same time as the debts, or deposits, are being made. Banks may only lend a certain percentage (*excess reserves*) of their demand deposits, which reserves are deposited at district Federal Reserve Banks. This is known as a "fractional reserve system" since only that portion of deposits not set aside by law as cash reserves may be used for lending.

Monetary policy is the managing of this supply of bank credit money. By controlling in certain technical ways the size of the member banks' excess reserves—from which loans to business can be made—the Federal Reserve can increase or decrease the capacity of banks to make loans and thus create money. Under inflationary conditions, monetary policy will require that reserves be decreased. This in turn will reduce lending and decrease the amount of checkbook money in circulation. It now becomes more expensive (with higher interest rates) and more difficult to borrow ("tight" money), thus serving to reduce spending. Since credit is more costly and more difficult to obtain, this will affect investments, the production of goods and employment, and the general level of prices.

By increasing bank reserves the Federal Reserve stimulates bank lending to consumers and businesses. Hence, during a recession this policy makes it easier to borrow at lower interest rates ("easy" money) for investing and spending, thus stimulating production and employment.

Monetary policy is effective in helping to prevent instability in the economy, but it is not a precise, never-failing instrument of policy with guaranteed results. A strong monetary policy can slow down a booming economy, but it canot guarantee to lower the level of prices. It is, of course, difficult to know exactly when to "tighten" or "loosen" bank reserves in order to adjust to predictions of inflation or recession. Spending and the creation of bank money do not follow easy formulas. Spending can be increased without the money supply rising if money is spent or turned over at a rapid rate. Easy money, too, does not insure borrowing, or its wise use. Monetary policy, unlike fiscal policy, involves less of the political process. It can be more quickly applied to changing situations. Promptness and precision, while desirable in both cases, are more easily obtained with monetary policy. Monetary policy, it must be remembered, works indirectly by affecting the cost and availability of credit.

Monetary policy *combined* with fiscal policy in the proper proportions constitutes the best medicine we possess today for combating economic instability. By coordinating "easy money" policies with government budget deficits and tax cuts, the economy can be given a strong push toward increasing total spending in recession periods to encourage recovery. Tight money, in collaboration with governmental budget surpluses and an increase in taxes, can help create an atmosphere of restraint on total spending when inflationary trends are blooming.

In meeting the challenge of keeping a dynamic market economy stable, while at the same time insuring full employment, our economic society has devised a number of worthy monetary and fiscal tools, together with improved statistical methods of measuring the economy's health. Determined never again to witness a Great Depression, which rendered 25 percent of the labor force jobless, and aware of the dangers of inflation, Americans are no longer willing to stand aside and let nature take its course. As one expert observed, "When the chips are down and economic expansion grinds to a halt, few spokesmen now appear before Congress, pleading for lower wages, less federal spending, or a balanced budget."

PART TWO

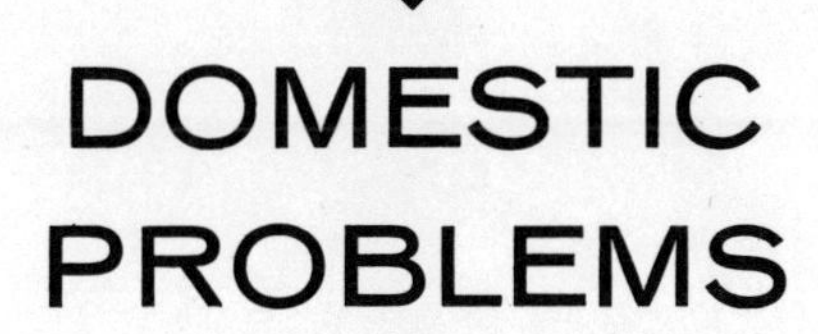

DOMESTIC PROBLEMS

CHAPTER 6

ECONOMIC GROWTH

Insuring the Nation's Future

Economic growth is a challenge for the simple reason that growing populations demand more and better goods and services for improving their standard of living. Meeting the increasing domestic needs (such as urban rehabilitation and better housing), solving the poverty problems, and fulfilling international commitments, (which include aid and defense) represent other aspects of this challenge. An important part of the challenge, furthermore, is the need to achieve economic growth while avoiding recessions or marked inflation.

Economic growth is the progressive increase in the total output of goods and services over a period of time. Since the measurement of this Gross National Product (GNP) is in terms of money, we must be sure to keep track of the changing record in terms of the changing value of the dollar. In other words, if the economic growth rate of 30 years ago is to be compared with today's, one must remember that goods and services for which we then paid 42 cents now cost one dollar. Therefore, we must value yesterday's production in terms of today's purchasing power in order to determine what has actually been accomplished. Using 1958 prices, we discover that 1938's GNP of $84.7 billion translates into $192.9 billion, while 1968's GNP of $860.7 becomes $706.9 billion—a difference of $514 billion rather than $776 billion!

ECONOMIC GROWTH IN THE UNITED STATES

In addition to evaluating the rate of economic growth in terms of *constant dollars* (dollar values that can be accurately compared), it also is necessary to consider differences in population for periods of economic growth. Thus in 1938 a population of some 130 million had a GNP of $84.7 million, while in 1968, 200 million people enjoyed a GNP of $860.7 million. By dividing the population into the current GNP you arrive at the *real growth per capita*, which is a more accurate measure of comparison. Thus for one hundred years the annual growth rate averaged 3 percent. During this same period the population increased annually by 1 percent. Therefore economists say that the real growth per capita rate is 2 percent.

At the outset it should be made clear that there is no magical percentage that qualifies as a country's optimum growth rate. Averages, for one thing, are deceptive and give false impressions of specific areas of the economy. The plastics industries may be thriving, while textiles may be in trouble. Moreover, averages also tell us little about quality changes or new products, such as electric refrigerators supplanting iceboxes, automobiles replacing buggies, or such new developments as television and miracle drugs. Furthermore, percentages do not tell us in what directions our economic growth should go. Do we want more luxuries or more social services, more defense items or more consumer goods, more consumer goods or more capital goods?

From its very beginnings, the United States has undergone economic growth. The British, albeit for their own interests, encouraged the colonies to pursue certain narrow goals of economic growth. They failed, as we know, to control the more general directions of the economic growth of the colonies, which were mainly along agricultural, mining, and shipping lines. The Industrial Revolution commenced a few decades before the Civil War, and has, of course, profoundly changed the nation's economic scene by making greater economic growth more feasible.

A quick glance at the record of economic growth of the United States in the last 50 years is revealing. Between 1916 and 1966 GNP rose about 1500 percent—from $48.9 billion to $740 billion. Income today (per capita, after taxes) is $2,400, more than double that of 1915, figured in terms of constant dollars. Similarly, average hourly earnings of factory workers have risen from 22 cents to $2.61, and average weekly earnings from $10.92 to $107.53. These advances were accomplished while the average workweek was being reduced from 49.4 to 41.2 hours. The United States has, in terms of Gross National Product, outdistanced its nearest rival, the Soviet Union, by a ratio of three to one. (See page 110 for the full GNP record.)

Why Are We Interested in Economic Growth?

If we move to more recent comparisons, we discover that production of goods and services from 1946 to 1965 almost doubled! Why then, it may be asked, is there any reason for concern? If we are so well off, why do we consider economic growth a problem? Strangely enough, one aspect of the problem stems from the fact that with great wealth it is easier for an economy to grow, but the reasons do not seem so apparent as they do in poorer countries. Dynamic systems such as ours also *must* advance, or fall behind.

There are more apparent reasons, however. While the totals—the GNP records—are impressive, the per capita returns are less so. Indeed, many pockets of poverty exist. And as we stated at the outset of this chapter, the basic reasons for economic growth revolve around the demands of our increasing population for higher levels of living and the need to fulfill international obligations. It also must be remembered that economic growth has not been a straight line of progress. True, the years from 1960 to 1968 witnessed unparalleled expansion. But economic growth has been hurt by severe depressions, recessions, wars, and other dislocations. Continued economic growth is necessary to make up for these past losses and to provide insurance for possible future calamities.

Let us now view in greater detail the specific reasons why we are interested in economic growth. We shall then turn to a discussion of conditions that promote and foster growth, followed by an investigation of ones that hinder it. Finally, we will consider "the price" we pay for growth.

With growth, all groups, including the poor, have a chance to better their standard of living from increased stocks of goods and services. This makes for a far easier solution to man's eternal quest to better himself materially than having economic groups battle each other over static production schedules. Hope rides on rising production curves; it toboggans when they flatten out and go downhill. From 1959–1966—years of good economic growth—the number of poor, nonfarm households dropped from 11.6 million to 10.3 million. This decline is directly related to the availability of good jobs at high wages.

Rising populations mean that there are more mouths to feed and bodies to care for. Yearly some 3½ million newborn babies scream their urgent demands upon the economy. Millions more older people retire—they both retire earlier and live longer than they used to—from their varied production tasks. Both groups, the young and the old, remain consumers and continue to look to the economy to fill their growing and increasing needs.

Unemployment, even in good times, remains at a level of 4 percent of the labor force. Keeping in mind the growing population, and the yearly entrance of millions of newcomers to job markets, we must run economically in order to stand still. Just to keep the unemployment rate to the 4 percent level, more than a million new jobs annually must be created! If we want to make inroads into the prevailing unemployment rate itself, the economy must grow even more. Remember, too, that increased productivity in various areas may be eliminating jobs. Therefore, even greater emphasis must be placed on the overall growth rate.

Though we may be swimming in a sea of prosperity, we are constantly in sight of problem islands. Who is not aware of the pressing urban problems that daily demand our attention: housing, slums, education, pollution, transportation, and welfare needs? Local governments are increasingly hard put to pay for the great demands for these public services. Minority groups, especially Negroes, need to come into the mainstream of the economy and out of the bogs in which they have for too long been economically depressed.

In recent years state and local government expenditures have risen rapidly. Total spending increased from $37 billion to $86 billion in the decade after 1956. This rate of spending represents an average annual increase of 9 percent, a percentage clearly above the GNP growth rate of 6 percent during the same period. Basically, this sharp spurt in spending reflects a growing demand for more and better services and (as we are all aware) the higher costs of providing them. Contributing to this demand on the state and local level are the steady increase in population, a growing number of children and older people requiring expensive social services, and a rapidly rising standard of living.

State and local spending is mainly devoted to purchases of goods and services, especially motor vehicles and other heavy equipment, payments to employees, and new construction of public buildings and highways. Purchases of goods and services by these governments alone amounted to 11 percent of the GNP in 1966. Not included in these purchases are the transfer payments, which cover pension fund benefits, old age assistance, aid to families with dependent children, and other programs. These payments, which have nearly doubled in the past decade, owe their increases mainly to the fact that more than 2 million additional cases have been added to the welfare rolls.

Education, however, still accounts for the largest proportion of expenditures by state and local governments—40 percent in fact. In the ten-year period after 1956, the educational budget shot up by 233 percent, from $13 billion to $34 billion.

There can be little doubt that the outlook is for continued increases in state and local spending. Despite the huge bill at present for education, there is obvious need for even better facilities. Few critics contest the need for tremendous improvements in urban transit and transportation. Yet the outlays necessary to put suggested changes into effect are stupendous. In this same category are the tremendous challenges that confront us in redeveloping the inner cities of our decaying urban centers.

Nor are these problem islands exclusively urban. Agriculture continues its tremendous technological displacement—every year hundreds of thousands of farmers are removed from production to become candidates for the nation's poverty rolls. Depressed industries, such as mining and textiles, dot the nation's economic map and leave families severely scarred by declining or nonexistent payrolls. Programs to alleviate these urban and rural problems demand private and public funds. Their ultimate improvement lies in the increase in the growth rate.

Economic growth also is required for another whole category of international needs: defense, prestige, and foreign aid. All these items share in common their dependence on current production. Whatever we spend in this category must be subtracted from what is available for civilian consumption *unless* we grow and thus provide for both areas.

Defense, for example, accounts for 10 percent of the GNP. Peacetime demands, the intercontinental ballistics missiles, the advanced supersonic model planes—in short, equipping men with today's electronic equipment—require great sums of money. Antiballistic missile defense systems are estimated to cost upward of $40 billion! When "little wars," such as the Korean and Vietnam conflicts are added, the defense figures mount astronomically. "Guns or butter?" is the classical way of phrasing the problem. Economic growth tells us that maybe you can plan for both, if necessary.

The United States occupies the foremost economic position in an increasingly interdependent world. Its dollar has supplanted the British pound as an international standard of value. Obviously, failure to grow economically will be reflected in the dollar's prestige, if not in a decline in trade and commerce between us and other nations.

We also are extremely conscious of our prestige in the many aspects of rivalry with the Soviet Union. Space probes, to take but one obvious area, are fantastically expensive. Servicing the less developed areas of the world is a worthy but formidable problem: helping to fight the evils of hunger, disease, and ignorance, as well as providing aid for the defense of selected nations. In the 20-year period since 1946 the total bill for foreign assistance has amounted to more than $122 billion.

While the 1967 expenditures for these services to other countries amounted to slightly less than 1 percent of that year's GNP, this amount also illustrates the difficulty of boosting the economy's growth rate. Increasing national output by even 1 percent, from, let us say, 3 to 4 percent requires a 33⅓ percent increase in the *rate* of growth. Hence it seems that the task of economic growth, as simple arithmetic indicates, is much greater than it first appears.

WHEN GROWTH FLOURISHES

Economic growth demands a favorable atmosphere if it is to flourish. A country's traditions must be receptive to increasing change; its government must be stable and encouraging; and its economic system must be extremely flexible and open to experiment.

Fortunately, the United States provides these basic ingredients for the growth of its economy. The history and culture of the country have conditioned the people to accept and, indeed, to expect frequent changes in their economy. Few traditions or customs impede changes. By contrast, the feudal backgrounds in some countries inhibit progress and innovation, as do certain mores, religious attitudes, and class and caste divisions prevalent in many underdeveloped countries of the world.

A stable government is an absolute requirement for growth. Business does not thrive in an atmosphere of tension, of uncertainty whether or not changing governmental policies will affect profits or even property. Needless to say, few of these concerns are present in the United States, regardless of shifts from Republican to Democratic administrations. In point of fact, government policies in the main are favorable to capital accumulation. Witness helpful fiscal and monetary policies, subsidy and tariff legislation for specific industries, tax incentives for growths, and investments in education and research and development.

The economic system must be enterprising and willing to take risks in accepting changes and innovations in products and in ways of producing them. America's entrepreneurs have repeatedly exhibited their numerous abilities along these lines. Labor, also, has demonstrated its talents and enterprise in learning new skills and in raising its level of education. America's consumers enter this picture, too, for they have consistently demonstrated their willingness to support the economy by buying "the new and improved," as they are constantly asked to do.

A growing population also has contributed toward a larger and diversified labor supply. And as we have seen, a rising population stimulates the production of more goods; it also places greater demands upon the nation's stock of resources.

In the long run, economic growth depends upon the ability to expand. Among the means of increasing growth are the advancement of knowledge and technology to better manage resources, the improvement in the education and skills of the work force, and the increase in capital equipment. Savings, of course, must be available to provide funds for these investments.

Economic growth has as one of its important ingredients the emphasis on research and development. Sufficient resources must be set aside to minimize the lag between a discovery and its industrial exploitation. (While the British discovered the relatively rare metal titanium in 1791, Americans only recently realized its uniquely light and durable values in the construction of airplanes.) One of the factors in the spectacular economic growth of the United States certainly has been the fact that R&D expense per capita is $94 as against $25 in Europe.

In addition to research and development, businessmen must readily accept risks in transferring ideas into reality. Curiously enough, many important European inventions have first been adapted for commercial purposes in America rather than in their country of origin. A very recent case in point is the application of the German concept of the variable dimension wing to the Boeing 2707 supersonic plane.

Efficient management techniques, creative and organizational ability are most important in mobilizing the many industrial forces necessary to give the economy its thrust into sustained growth.

Technological advance has been called "the natural star actor in the drama of economic growth." As demand for natural resources has risen, new technology has increased the capacity to meet this demand. The cost of raw materials, when compared with other costs, has increased very slowly in the past 100 years, and the cost of some items has not increased at all. Reasons for this favorable development revolve around the opening of new sources of supply, the use of substitute materials, more importing of needed resources, and a greater efficiency in the use of materials.

Between 1914 and 1950 the United States alone used up more

fuels and other minerals than the entire world had consumed up to that time. Remember that a modern economy functions as a provider of raw materials *and* as a consumer. However, the problem in this country is not one of excessive consumption but better management (economizing) in the use of raw materials and better government policies toward this end. The real problem remains one of finding ways through diversified technology of keeping down costs of resources and for finding substitutes. This calls for increased expenditures for research and development by industry and government.

Of late, economists have come to realize that investment in education is a vital factor in economic growth. One prominent authority in this field estimates that education may have contributed as much as 20 percent to the nation's economic growth from 1929–1957. The economic function of a nation's educational system is to build human capital by increasing the capacity of innate abilities to help improve production. "No country can enjoy economic growth unless it relies heavily on educated citizens," is the advice of a recent Department of Commerce publication. While statistics indicate a large increase in our educational investment, the complex needs of our economy continue to make even greater demands.

Capital investments go to the heart of the problem of economic growth. As we discovered in an earlier chapter, it is the improved tools, machinery, and equipment and that permit workers to increase their productivity. Again, to substantially raise output workers must produce more for every man-hour of work. Tremendous increases in capital equipment, investments in plant and equipment based upon improved technology, understandably have played a great role in pushing the GNP in recent years to unprecedented heights.

Savings from current production are needed for the investments that will increase the growth of total output. In recent years 65 percent of this output has gone for private consumption as compared to the 35 percent that has been allocated to investment and government expenditures. We know that additional savings are needed for additional investments. "What we don't know," points out a former member of the President's Council of Economic Advisers, "is whether consumption will have to be restricted to 60 percent of total output, say, or even 50 percent, in order to increase the growth rate of a fully employed economy by 1 percentage point." Thus, while increased savings are undoubtedly needed for increased investments for greater production, many factors in the current performance of the economy must be considered.

Along with the factors that stimulate economic growth, there are factors that work to slow down growth. Labor and management may not be sufficiently mobile. Either through ignorance or lack of interest both groups may hesitate to move to other industries or other geographic regions where opportunities are better. Sometimes monopolies maintain high prices or fail to push new products or improve their production methods. Similarly, labor unions at times practice restrictive policies by keeping new members out of certain industries or by fighting the introduction of new machinery.

Tariffs and government subsidies often support inefficient industries, which then have no incentive for improvement. Other governmental policies may be harmful, such as the promotion of high interest rates or unfair tax rates. Excessive inflation also can unsettle the economy, as can recessions or depressions, and thus interfere with growth.

Consumers may fail to save, or save too much, creating a situation where sufficient funds for investment may not be available. Workers may decide that they value leisure and a shorter working week more than increased income and additional work. Population may grow too slow to provide workers and consumers, or it may grow too fast and outpace productivity gains. Minority groups may be deprived of their fair share of jobs and income, thus denying the economy badly needed resources. Research and development may not be pushed sufficiently, or results properly exploited. Total consumer and productive demand must keep pace to absorb increases in production. Investment spending must also keep up with increased savings in a growth economy. Finally, it is natural to expect a slowdown in the economy as the slack of unused resources becomes absorbed; indeed sometimes it is necessary to encourage a slowdown in order to prevent a disorderly scramble for scarce resources and to prevent prices from rising too quickly.

Paying for Growth

The "costs" of economic growth essentially boil down to the question of how much we want to sacrifice in the present for how much we expect to gain in the future. This involves a balancing, or even a juggling, of costs now versus opportunities later. Do we want to spend all our income today, or save some for tomorrow's expected pleasures? Or is tomorrow too far away? Do we settle for income now and leisure later? Do we encourage growth at the risk of unsettling the economy with inflation or recession? Do we introduce new machinery, new methods, and new products, at the risk of depressing some industries and certain areas and displacing and idling workers? Do we accept crowded cities, depressed and overexpanded areas, loss of certain skills, growing concentrations of big business and big labor for future better standards of living? Do we emphasize private consumption at the expense of society's needs for better schools, hospitals, public transportation, and protection?

Walter W. Heller, former Chairman of the Council of Economic Advisers, in his *New Dimensions of Political Economy* sums up the liabilities in the balance of economic growth in this way: "First claim on the *products* of growth should be to repair the ravages of the growth *process.* If as *by-products* in our quest for growth, we destroy the purity of our air and water, generate ugliness and social disorder, displace workers and their skills, gobble up our natural resources, and chew up the amenities in and around our cities, the repair of that damage should have first call on the proceeds of growth."

Over the long run economic growth is marked by an expansion of investment, consumption, job opportunities, higher living standards, and greater leisure for the average worker. Over short periods, however, job opportunities have not always expanded enough to match the increased number of people seeking work, including those workers displaced by labor-saving technology.

Above all, economic growth must be weighed in the light of what we consider to be our social goals and national purpose. As a famous historian posed this problem: "In all this, in the evolution of the greatest industrial society that the world has ever seen, have we gained or have we lost? Are men and women today happier and better off, politically, spiritually, mentally, morally, and physically, than our ancestors were. . .?"

In any event, the evidence of successful economic growth in the United States is apparent to all. With only 7 percent of the world's land area, and 6 percent of the world's population, we produce 33 percent of the world's goods and services, utilizing 33 percent of the world's electrical energy. We obviously aim to continue steering a resolute course toward increased economic growth that will assure a rising standard of living for growing numbers of Americans and that will insure the fulfillment of our international obligations. The Employment Act of 1946 pledges the federal government to this goal by directing it to give specific consideration to ways of achieving and maintaining a high level of employment.

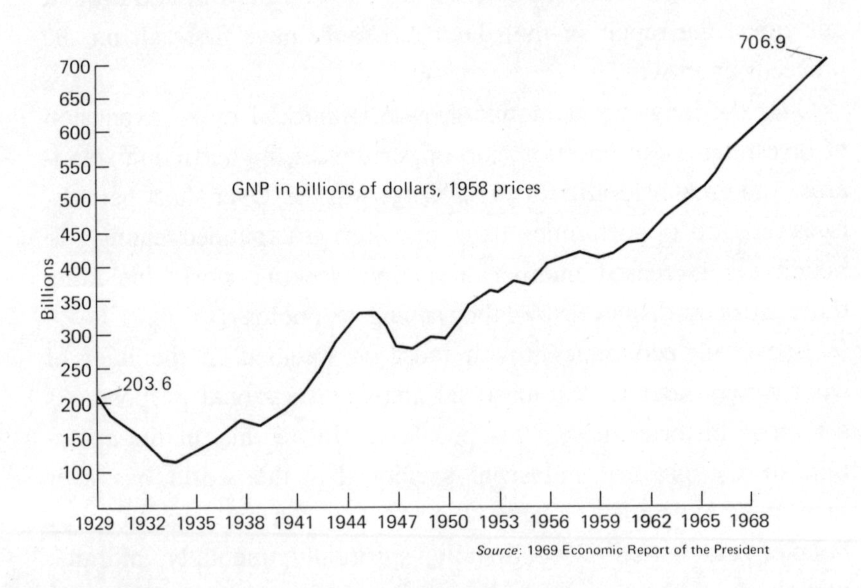

Fig. 7. The growth of the U.S. Gross National Product from 1923 to present.

CHAPTER 7

PERSONAL ECONOMIC SECURITY

Individual Welfare and the Economy

The challenge of personal economic security poses the problem of how best to provide for those who, for various reasons, fail to share adequately in the nation's prosperity. Included in this category of need are those who suffer from the loss of income, or whose income is inadequate: the unemployed, the aged, the disabled or handicapped, the broken family, the poorly educated, and the victims of discrimination. An awakened social conscience is now focused on the need to help that one eighth of the U.S. population that remains in a condition of poverty. We are repeatedly reminded, through mass demonstrations and reports in the daily press, of the stark conditions of starvation and malnutrition under which many of the poor live—conditions that contrast sharply with the increasingly comfortable standards most Americans enjoy.

Aside from the humanitarian aspect of personal security, we must be concerned with the impact of welfare programs on the economy. There remains the ever-present practical need to use more fully the nation's precious human resources for continued economic growth. We must consider the costs of benefits for unemployment, old age, and welfare—and their impact on the economy. We must consider not only the costs, in terms of what the economy can afford, but we must also be aware that improved incomes will turn a significant portion of the population into more normal members of the economy. After all, the economic community is not really healthy when some of its members cannot afford a minimally decent standard of living.

Personal economic security for the average American means an income that makes it possible for him to maintain a decent standard of living and to provide—with Social Security help—for layoffs and old age. Fortunately, the majority of citizens have now achieved these goals, thanks to rising productivity. Real GNP (in terms of constant dollars) grew by $182 from 1961 to 1967, for a rise of nearly 38 percent, or more than 5 percent per year. In this favorable economic atmosphere, persons living in poverty fell from 38.9 million in 1959 to 29.7 million in 1966. (Poverty, as defined by the federal government, is roughly $3,553 a year or lower for an average nonfarm family of four.) Keeping in mind the increase in population during this period of time, a decrease in poverty by almost 7 percent (from 22.1 to 15.4 percent) is indeed remarkable progress, even if a long road remains to be traversed. (In 1969 the number of poor people had been reduced to 25 million, about 13 percent of the nation's population.)

Personal economic security, it would seem, under an expanding economy is becoming less of a problem for more of our people. While this statement is true, it merits further investigation. An expanding economy means a changing economy, but it also signifies uneven and unsettling growth. While some industries, occupations, and regions bustle with expansionist energy, others are declining, failing, or being transformed, with all the personal anguish that accompanies this type of change. Under these circumstances, personal economic security can be endangered, and the individual reduced to a poverty level. Thus the process of growth that serves to reduce poverty sometimes acts to create it.

Poverty and unemployment go to the heart of many problems in our society. Their causes are complex, as a mere listing of governmental efforts to alleviate these problems will attest. In addition to basic manpower programs, Social Security, and public assistance programs, there are plans for health, regional economic development, housing, urban redevelopment and community facilities, school lunches, and various food distribution activities. Obviously, to attack any problem as broad and complicated as poverty and unemployment requires an expert meshing of the many programs mentioned.

For these expenditures more than $27 billion was appropriated in 1967–1968. (Federal aid to the poor in 1960 was $9.5 billion.) That was 27 percent of all federal nondefense cash payments. Direct relief payments to maintain basic minimum needs for this period alone equaled $3 billion as Washington's contribution for the "federal–state public assistance program." In addition, $2 billion was provided by state and local governments for needy families and individuals—the indigent, the aged, the blind, the disabled, and families with dependent children. This latter type of welfare, usually known as "home relief," is provided solely by local and state funds.

Public assistance has grown to the point where it has been called "the greatest domestic problem in the United States." Indeed, in 1967 the New York State Commissioner of Social Welfare declared that "this economic and social segregation of a huge, growing segment of the population from the mainstream of living must end." In pointing out the state's bill of more than $1 billion for a year of welfare assistance to almost 1 million people (1 out of 17 state residents) he further commented: "No economy, however affluent, can afford the rising social and financial costs of a situation in which the resources of great numbers of its people are not developed and not used, in which the promise of a decent, wholesome, self-sufficient maturity is virtually denied to millions of its children."

OUR CONCERN WITH PERSONAL ECONOMIC SECURITY

How can we account for this growing concern for personal economic security in an era of unprecedented economic growth and prosperity?

To a great extent the answers lie in the changes that have brought the United States to a society overwhelmingly industrialized and urbanized with unprecedented high standards of living. Four out of five people in today's labor force make a living working for others. They are dependent upon others for wages and salaries; their loss of jobs brings them face to face with the terror of economic insecurity. In the early days of the republic, 90 percent of the nation's people lived on self-sufficient farms. In this predominantly rural society, the family, with occasional help from private charity, was generally able to provide for those who needed support. Today, not only has the farm population shrunk to less than 6 percent, but the entire population has multiplied fiftyfold. With 200 million people, all social problems, including personal economic security, have a way of multiplying!

A healthy expanding economy will effectively allay fears of personal economic insecurity for most citizens. But prosperity alone will not comfort many other millions. Unfortunately, the aged, the infirm, and many husbandless mothers benefit little from economic growth because they are outside the labor market. They are kept out by highly visible sentries: illiteracy, lack of skills, racial discrimination, and ill health. Others are able to obtain employment but their skills are so meager that their earnings prevent them from leaving the category of the poor. In fact, a surprisingly large number of the poor have some kind of a job but they need higher skills and better productivity rates in order to increase their income.

For those with inadequate skills, who hover at the edges of the employment market and those who find the gates closed to them, prosperity alone offers no golden key to increased income. Improved manpower policies with effective training programs are needed that will permit marginal and submarginal workers to be welcomed into the labor markets. Rational and humane income maintenance programs—money supplied by the government—also are essential to combat poverty and unemployment.

Those in dependency age brackets—under 18 and over 65—now constitute 45 percent of the total population, and since more than 70 percent of the population presently lives in urban surroundings, the problems are compounded. For as the "bill" for welfare aid mounts—in any month about 7½ million people are wholly or partially dependent on public relief—the cities find it increasingly difficult to meet ever-mounting costs. In New York City the cost for welfare has supplanted education as the biggest expense item, consuming 26 percent of the budget. As the proportion of dependents rises in the cities, the proportion of taxpayers who ultimately pay the bill dwindles, thus creating serious budgetary problems. Consider just one statistic: Fifty years ago three-fourths of the Negroes—an obviously deprived group—lived in rural country, but today three-fourths live in urban areas. In 1968 roughly one-fifth of New York City's Negroes (and one-fourth of its Puerto Ricans) depended upon public assistance.

Remember, too, that today's cities greet newcomers with millions of substandard dwellings, rising crime and delinquency rates, deteriorating commercial areas, increasingly polluted atmospheres, vast traffic and transportation problems, and widespread social unrest. President Johnson in his Economic Report for 1967 said that cities are "in trouble" because, "Most cities cannot afford the massive expenditures necessary to solve these problems. The flight of higher income families and businesses to the suburbs erodes sources of revenue for the cities, even as expenditure demands escalate."

Between 1960 and 1966 state and local governments increased their expenditures by 65 percent, the majority of which were spent on social services. Municipalities continually complain—with much truth—that since the problems of personal economic security are to a considerable extent national in scope, it follows that there should be more national responsibility and aid in settling these problems. There is a large body of expert opinion that holds that the cities are financially incapable of making any serious inroads in the area of personal economic security.

In this discussion of personal economic security problems, we will next consider three broad categories: unemployment, needy old age, and various types of public assistance.

THE PROBLEM OF UNEMPLOYMENT

"Unemployment," President John F. Kennedy warned, "is our number one economic problem. It wastes the lives of men and women, depriving both them and the nation." While it is easy to agree with this statement, it is not so easy to agree on the best solution to it.

Stated boldly, our economy must create 1 million new job openings yearly *in addition* to those created by retirements, deaths, disability, and other normal reasons, merely to take care of young people entering the labor market. When there are idle hands, and the wheels of industry are not fully turning, it is possible by various measures to increase demand, while reducing unemployment and maintaining prices at a reasonably stable level. But as recent experience in a prosperous period indicates, a reduction in the unemployment rate to below 4 percent of the labor force (about 3 million unemployed)—spurred by the war in Vietnam—may help to raise prices to a "clearly unacceptable rate." Thus it seems that when the economy is going full blast, a sudden reduction in unemployment can contribute to an inflationary rise. It should be added, however, that society may be willing to pay an inflationary price for a lower rate of unemployment.

Unemployment is always with us, even during so-called "good times." During recessions, of course, the rate rises considerably. Fortunately, a repetition of the record unemployment of the Great Depression of the 1930s now seems unlikely. For 10 years one out of every five workers was unemployed, and at one point nearly 13 million—a fourth of the labor force—were jobless. Indeed, it was this devastating experience, in which private, local, and state agencies proved helpless, that marked the first occasion in our nation's history when the federal government took active and positive steps to alleviate widespread economic suffering.

The President's Council of Economic Advisers considers 4 percent unemployment a reasonable goal. (The graph indicates this figure has not been achieved too often in the past decade.) While this figure can be disputed, it does not mean that zero unemployment is possible. Experts agree that a certain amount of unemployment is necessary in a market economy to permit workers to quit jobs and to allow employers to discharge them. Then, too, many businesses are continually expanding or contracting, while others need workers on a seasonal basis. This floating labor force, which averages 3 percent of the work force, stands in the wings, waiting to play its part in the ever-changing economic scene.

Types of Unemployment: Frictional and Structural

Let us take a closer look at the nearly 3 million unemployed at the end of 1967. Perhaps two-thirds were moving between jobs (*frictional unemployment*); for example, new entrants looking for a job; those who quit one job to look for another; persons seasonally unemployed; and workers temporarily laid off. The remaining third are the "hard-core" unemployed, who will have a considerable wait for a steady job. This group of unemployed is a problem because they lack the necessary skills of education for regular work;

Fig. 8. Employment and rate of unemployment. (See appendix table 7.)

they are victims of past or present discrimination; they are either unable or unwilling to move from depressed areas and occupations; and they are physically or emotionally handicapped.

Further study reveals a darker picture behind the above statistics. Another half million to one million *potential* workers were not even counted as unemployed. Many had long ago abandoned any search for a job. Some had never tried. Another 2 million breadwinners—particularly the poorly skilled—did not earn enough to support their families in a minimum standard of decent subsistence. Finally, 6½ million poor families had heads of households unable to work. These ranks were filled with the aged, the severely handicapped, and the widowed or deserted mothers with young children.

During times of prosperity, unemployment is heavily concentrated among the unskilled, the poorly educated, those with poor work habits, and the poorly motivated. Any increase in demand in good times will result in a call for a cross section of workers ranging from professionals, to skilled, semiskilled, and even unskilled. At this particular time, however, the unemployed do not represent a cross section of the population, being overrepresented in the unskilled and the poorly educated categories. Hence we have an anomalous situation of joblessness in a "help-wanted" era.

Broadly speaking, there are two general reasons for unemployment which to a considerable extent complement each other. Here we are speaking of those who are willing and able to work but for whom the economy does not provide jobs. One reason is a lagging rate of economic growth caused by an inadequate consumer demand and an insufficient business investment. The task here is to raise the level of economic activity. This can be stimulated by either private spending (aided by tax cuts) or by increased government spending. The other general reason for unemployment is called *structural.* As the heading indicates, basic changes in industry sometimes decrease the opportunities for employment.

Another cause for unemployment involves the difficulties of individuals adjusting to the job market. Thus there are a host of reasons for joblessness: elimination of jobs by technological change; depressed areas where a dominant industry has declined or moved away; racial discrimination (the unemployment rate is more than twice as high for Negroes as it is for whites); and inadequate training or education.

"Invisible" or "hidden" unemployment must also be included in the structural and hard-core area of unemployment. A special study by the Department of Labor revealed that the unemployment rate was close to 10 percent in urban slums, compared to 3.7 percent (February 1967) for the entire nation. Many other slum dwellers considered employed were working only part time. Still others had become so discouraged that they gave up the search for work, thus avoiding statistical enrollment in the ranks of the unemployed. "No conceivable increase in the Gross National Product would stir these backwaters," concluded the study.

It can scarcely be denied that combating hard-core unemployment calls for retraining, job finding, and job-creation programs. Communications in the labor market also are faulty. According to one expert, "The channels by which workers learn about job vacancies and employers know about available qualified workers could stand considerable improvement."

Help for the Unemployed

In recent years the federal government has provided training and retraining aimed at developing this unused or underutilized talent in the labor force, with emphasis on the disadvantaged. Included in its program (described in Chapter 4) are the Manpower development and Training Act (MDTA), which provides special assistance for intensive on-the-job training for disadvantaged and other persons. In 1968 close to 600,000 persons were enrolled in its various programs. A Neighborhood Youth Corps program aids needy youths in school and trains dropouts. Training and work experience for disadvantaged youth are provided by the Job Corps. Other programs include an adult work program and a special program for retraining and employing residents of blighted areas.

A Federal Unemployment Tax Act (on employers only) provides benefits for a limited period of time for qualified workers in commerce and industry who become unemployed. Although benefits vary, since the states enforce their own regulations, payments usually are given for 26 weeks. Aside from the obvious needs of the unemployed, these benefits have been credited with providing needed purchasing power during times of recession, thus helping to improve the state of the economy. As a built-in stabilizer, it has been recommended that extended benefits for the long-term unemployed be coupled with automatic access to training and retraining and other rehabilitative services.

Two private plans to alleviate unemployment continue to attract attention. The Guaranteed Annual Wage (GAW) insures workers a definite number of workweeks at regular wages. Supplementary Unemployment Benefits (SUB) are tied in with unemployment insurance benefits. Provision is usually made for the worker to receive two-thirds of his regular pay, based upon the unemployment insurance benefits he normally would receive, and an additional amount contributed by employers from their special SUB fund.

THE PROBLEM OF JOBLESS OLD AGE

Even if one is assured employment throughout his working life, he still must consider the need to provide for his old age. Thanks to the marvels of modern medicine, a greater portion of the population now reach old age. On the average, more than a generation (20 years) has been added to life expectancy in the twentieth century. Men can now expect to live until 70, while women can look forward to an additional 5 years of life. However, extended life does not necessarily mean prolonged earning power, nor does it insure sufficient savings for the expenses of jobless old age.

Generally the older person, especially if he is over 65, finds it difficult to keep his job or, if discharged, to obtain a new one. Most persons beyond the age of 65, therefore, have no alternative but to depend upon their pensions. A 1967 study sponsored by the Social Security Administration (Department of Health, Education and Welfare) revealed that the income of 50 percent of the families, in which at least one member was 65 or over, fell below $3,000. The retired person's income suffers from a continual inflation of his fixed income, which has only been partially offset by recent Social Security benefit increases. Pensioners also are excluded from the "gains of productivity"—the higher income that goes to workers and investors. "If our society cannot or will not employ them at prevailing wages," concluded the study, "then the only alternative is a higher pension—one with a built-in escalator that will keep the pension at a level of not less than 75 percent of prevailing wages."

Whether or not one agrees that this proposal should be adopted, the fact remains that security for old age is becoming more of a problem, rather than less of a problem. More than 20 million individuals in 1967 were over 65, and by 1975 the number will have increased to 31 million. Viewed as individuals, rather than as members of family groups, almost three-fourths have no income of their own or have less than $1,000 a year. We have alluded to the limited opportunities to supplement income in old age. (Keep in mind the fact that more than half of those employed at age 65 retire.) While some needs decrease at this age, other expenses, such as medical needs, increase sharply.

Security in Old Age

Individuals may attempt to secure their future with personal savings (including bank accounts, stocks, and bonds), insurance, and real estate. However, these provide assurances of varying amounts of income for only a limited number. By far the overwhelming number of retired people depend upon private pensions or Social Security benefits, or a combination of both.

Company-sponsored pension systems have increased tremendously since World War II. At present about 25 million, or about 30 percent of the labor force, are enrolled in systems that also often include various welfare benefits such as hospitalization, life insurance, and medical aid. As a rule, pensions to which only the company contributes aim to give workers at retirement 40 to 50 percent of their regular pay. Procedures, however, vary greatly from company to company, making it difficult to generalize about private pensions.

Old Age, Survivors, Disability and Health Insurance (OASDHI, but more commonly called Social Security) inaugurated in 1935, now covers 90 percent of the work force. Both employer and employee contribute 4.4 percent each of wages up to $7,800 annually. (Increases decreed in the present law will eventually raise the combined rate to 11.8 percent by 1987.) Retirement benefits commence at age 62. (Men may secure more if they wait until 65.) There are also special benefits for disability and for burial expenses. *Medicare*, a hospital insurance plan for those over 65, was added in 1966. A voluntary supplemental medical aid plan also is available for $3 a month. *Medicaid*, a federal–state-supported program of medical care, is offered to welfare clients and those classified as medically indigent.

There can be little doubt about the importance of OASDHI, in addition to private pension plans and personal savings, in helping to provide peace of mind for the security of workers in their old age. Few of the aged, it should be added, have supplemental sources of income. Only about 15 percent of those over 65, for instance, are now receiving private pension pay. About 40 percent have assets of less than $1,000. In 1967, benefits for all beneficiaries were increased by 13 percent, making the minimum amount $55 a month.

Old Age Insurance under the Social Security Act remains the basic retirement system for most of the labor force. OASDHI benefits in 1967 totaled $27 billion for more than 23 million beneficiaries. Roughly one-third of these benefits went to the poor, and another two-fifths went to households that would otherwise have been poor. These benefits, which are generally used for the purchase of necessities, quickly make their way into the economic stream, thus helping to keep it moving. It is estimated that 30 percent of the aged would suffer from poverty were not it for Social Security. Two million elderly now living below the poverty line would drop even deeper into the slough whose name is "despond." Nearly two-fifths of all the aged remain poor. About 15 percent of the population over 65 receives no benefits at all under the Social Security system, while only 10 percent receives the present maximum allowance of $218 a month. Still, this system must be credited with contributing to the encouraging reduction of poverty among aged householders, from 46 percent in 1959 to 37 percent in 1966.

Since new retirees will be entitled to greater benefits as a result of the recent higher wage rates and recent increased benefits, the general situation for the aged should improve. Inflation, however, still remains a deadly foe of those receiving Social Security benefits. For example, in the 7-year period after 1959 the budget ($3,044) for a retired couple in the New York area rose more than 40 percent. During the same period, however, Social Security benefits increased by only a little more than 20 percent. Obviously, under these conditions a couple would need savings or other income to supplement their shrinking Social Security dollars. Further liberalization in benefits—particularly in minimum benefits—geared to today's realities, rather than the depression standards that prevailed when Social Security was born, can hasten the day when all Americans will be assured upon retirement of a pension adequate to prevent poverty.

THE PROBLEM OF PUBLIC ASSISTANCE

Public assistance is the major income maintenance program aimed directly at the poor. It includes cash payments for old age (not covered by OASDHI), death or absence of the breadwinner, disability, and blindness. Standards of eligibility are established by the individual states, which pay 41 percent of the costs. Less than half of the poor qualify for aid under public assistance; only

22 percent, as a result of difficult state eligibility requirements, actually receive any help. Even those who qualify receive inadequate payments.

More than 7 million now receive public assistance, of whom it is estimated less than one percent are capable of going to work. It is further estimated that only about 50,000 fathers capable of learning to support themselves and their families are on relief. By far the largest public assistance program is the Aid to Families with Dependent Children (AFDC) which includes 3 million children and 1 million adults.

An interesting experiment in attempting to develop incentives (albeit one that aroused considerable controversy) has recently been introduced into the AFDC program. A 1967 amendment to the Social Security Act requires certain employables in this program to take jobs or to undergo training. Guidelines set by the Department of Health, Education and Welfare for the work incentive program involve persons 16 years or older in the AFDC program, except for those who have health or various other problems. Eligibles may be assigned to basic or vocational education, work experience programs, special work projects, or on-the-job training. Those who are given employment will be permitted to retain the first $30 of their monthly earnings and one-third of the remainder of the pay without deductions being made from welfare grants.

In some states families are ineligible for relief if there is an employed, or employable, adult male although he may be unable to provide adequately for his family. Only by deserting the family can he make them eligible for cash payments. Another grave defect of public assistance is that welfare recipients are not permitted to earn more than small amounts of money without suffering equivalent deductions from welfare checks. Thus self-support and the encouragement of incentives is stifled. Endless red tape and complicated bookkeeping also serve to tie the hands of social workers, who too often perform clerical and policing, rather than professional, functions. In general, welfare programs are costly to administer; yet standards remain low and uneven. And their general approach to the poor has not changed much from medieval times.

The blight of poverty is unevenly distributed throughout the land and among its people. It is disproportionately visible in the central cities, in certain rural nonfarm districts, and in various agricultural areas. (Farm poverty, it should be emphasized, is especially serious since most of the farm poor remain ineligible for income-maintenance programs.) Poverty also is unevenly concentrated throughout the population. It disproportionately strikes the aged, nonwhites, and members of households headed by women. Thus a larger fraction of the poor are found in these categories than are encountered in other elements of the general population.

Most poor households have no full-time earner to help them stay out of poverty. The fact that there are 10½ million people in poor households with working age males provokes ready reactions in some about those who seemingly prefer welfare to work. A brief acquaintance with some of the vital statistics of poverty should provide some insight into the accuracy of this charge. Households without full-time earners are mainly headed by persons over 65 (30 percent) or by women or disabled men under 65 (30 percent).

Households with a fully employed male head make up less than 20 percent of the poor. Nearly 1¾ million families in 1965 were poor in spite of the fact that the head of the family was employed full time during the year. About 700,000 of these families had four or more children. Another 1.5 million poor families had a male head who suffered from severe unemployment. And, again, they make up the legions under the unglamorous banners of the unskilled, the poorly educated, and the poorly motivated. Particularly difficult to pull out of poverty are the nonfarm households headed by women. For while 20 percent of nonfarm households headed by men graduated from the ranks of poverty between 1959 and 1966, only 2 percent of women-dominated households made the transition. Nearly one-half of all poor households continues to be headed by women.

At present, 4 million poor households headed by an able-bodied male under 65 (who is an inadequate breadwinner) are ineligible for public assistance. They need benefits that will help them to end the poverty cycle in which a blighted environment denies their children the skills and the attitudes they need to break out of poverty as adults. For the longer run, the Council of Economic Advisers suggests that "education, training, health and rehabilitation services, counseling, employment information, and other supportive services are the key escape routes from poverty for potential full-time workers with inadequate earning capacity."

In recent years much critical attention has been focused on the desirability of providing benefits on the basis of need, without degrading investigations, while promoting incentives for self-help. A much-discussed proposal would grant a minimum income allowance, or a negative income tax. Under this system the federal government would make up the difference in any year for all families whose income fell below $3,553. Professor Milton Friedman's proposals for a negative income tax have received more attention than any other plans along these lines. Stemming as they do from one of the nation's leading laissez-faire economists, these ideas have had a profound impact upon all concerned with the glaring shortcoming of present welfare systems. Essentially the negative income tax method calls for everyone to file an income tax report. In cases where incomes are below the level of taxation, individuals would be compensated by the federal government in order to guarantee a certain minimum income that would bring them above the poverty level.

How far the spirit of welfare reform has permeated national thinking was recently illustrated by the Nixon Administration's proposal to make a minimum standard of $1600 annually in federal aid available to all needy families with children, regardless of the father's employment status. Declarations of need, with spot checks like those used for income tax returns, would replace the present demeaning methods of investigation. Minimum nationwide standards would abolish the present monthly range of benefits for families in similar situations, from $39 in Mississippi to $263 in New Jersey. Despite considerable criticism about the limited minimum standard, and other specifics, the principles of national standards and greater federal assumption of responsibility for welfare were widely hailed.

Ease of operation gives this scheme an appeal that few poverty programs can match. But the objections to general acceptance of the revolutionary doctrine of the negative income tax—giving out money on such a large scale for not working—are legion. Regardless of the intrinsic value of this proposal, there are serious objections that would have to be overcome, objections rooted in the psychological, historical, and cultural backgrounds of this country. For example, how would those barely above the minimum level react to working for an income when almost as much could be received from the government for doing nothing? As Wilber J. Cohen, former Secretary of Health, Education and Welfare, pointed out, before the negative income tax could be accepted, it would have to be part of "a package plan that brings income and training and jobs, [that shows] how to budget, [and] how to live in urban society, [and how to be] getting the kinds of services that [the recipients] need."

Less spectacular than the negative income tax, but more closely akin to the family allowances of other nations, is economist James Tobin's plan for a *guaranteed annual income*. This scheme would award all families below the $3,553 "poverty line" allowances of $400 for each member of the family, with $150 granted for the fifth and sixth child. Subsidies would be reduced by 40 percent for each additional dollar earned, with the proviso that no further grants would be made to families that succeeded in earning $5,000 a year.

In evaluating personal economic security, we must consider the matter of incentives, if sufficient cash support were offered to raise each poor household's income to a fixed minimum. Who will take the lower-paying jobs? What will happen to certain occupations and certain areas? Does everyone have a right to a specified income whether he is *unable* to earn or *unwilling* to work? There also are vital questions to answer regarding the increasing centralization of power at the federal level and the effect upon the economy in handling the fantastic labyrinth of welfare programs. Serious doubts also may be cast on the value of many of the federal programs, especially those poorly administered, in actually overcoming poverty.

We must strive for a more humane and generous welfare system for aiding the poor. Cash benefits programs, for the present, would seem to be essential for the personal economic security of the hard-core poor. We should remember, however, that it is easier to give individuals money than to turn them into productive and self-respecting citizens. We must continue to improve social insurance programs. We must strive to increase our rate of economic growth and thus provide jobs for the poor who are able to work full time. Significant reductions in poverty, as we frequently noted, occur only when the economy is expanding. Expanded training programs will be increasingly needed to effectively prepare the disadvantaged for the world of work. Above all, economic opportunity for better jobs and better housing must remain open to all citizens.

The question is not, as a former member of the Council of Economic Advisers remarked, "whether we can afford to transfer as much as 3 percent of our GNP [to the poor]. The question is whether, in the name of equity and humanity, tranquillity and harmony, we can afford to do less." Or as the Report of the National Commission on Technology, Automation and Economic Progress concluded, "The needs of our society provide ample opportunities to fulfill the promise of The Employment Act of 1964: 'A job for all those able, willing, and seeking to work.' "

George Bernard Shaw couched his warning about the dangers of poverty in noneconomic terms, but the warning is nevertheless cogent:

> Security, the chief pretense of civilization, cannot exist where the worst of dangers, the danger of poverty, hangs over everyone's head. All the other crimes are virtues beside it. . . . It degrades the poor and infects with its degradation the whole neighborhood in which they live. And whatever can degrade a neighborhood can degrade a country and a continent and finally a whole civilization.

An affluent society, whose advertisements for dog and cat food would whet the appetites of the world's starving masses, needs to be reminded of Shaw's warning. It also can take heed of its own accomplishments. Removing 19 million people from poverty in 7 years (1961–1968) and insuring them better housing, better nutrition, better medical care, and more years of schooling for their children is surely an achievement worthy of further intensified endeavors.

PART THREE

INTERNATIONAL PROBLEMS

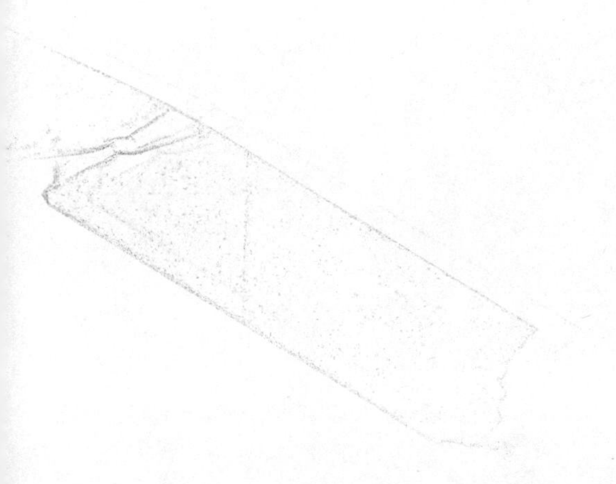

CHAPTER 8

INTERNATIONAL ECONOMICS

Trade and Investments Abroad

International economics deals with the problems of trade and investments among the nations of the world. The key to understanding the many complications of this subject is the realization that a country's dealings in trade and investments, since they concern other nations, can never be regulated like local traffic, for example, where a city manager may decree one-way streets.

The challenge of international economics has been dramatically described by a recent Secretary of Commerce: "We in the United States must understand and appreciate in all its ramifications the full meaning of the global market concept. It means, for one thing, the American domestic market—the greatest and most lucrative in the world—is no longer the private preserve of the American businessman. We are but one corner, one segment of that market." This challenge of international economics essentially reduces itself to the problem of finding ways and means of increasing our trade and investments abroad. It also calls for an understanding of the obstacles blocking this expansion.

Basically, the United States is involved in world economic issues because of the gigantic size and strength of its economy. As the leading political power of the free world, it also has vital interests in maintaining the stability of its industrialized allies and in helping the developing countries improve their economies. Thus international economics is inevitably linked up with national interest and foreign policy. As a nation, we can no more refrain from international dealings than a state can avoid business relations with the federal government.

THE WORLD'S LARGEST EXPORTER

Not surprsingly—since it produces 33 percent of the world's goods and services—the United States is the world's largest exporter. Between 1953 and 1967 world trade expanded by almost 2½ times. Since the United States contributes 18 percent of the goods in the world's export market, it has, understandably, greatly profited from this spectacular growth in trade.

In actual figures, this country's exports ($33.6 billion in 1968) add up to only 4 percent of its GNP, but like all figures, they bear closer inspection. These figures tell us little, for example, about the dependence of many foreign factories on American-made machinery; they do not hint at worldwide need for American-made farm equipment; they do not detail the food products that add variety to the daily life of others, nor the medicines and drugs that help to sustain that life.

While the nation's exports average only 4 percent of its GNP, exports for particular industries often represent a greater percentage. Agriculture, for example, has a heavy stake in the export market. In 1966, 17 percent of the total farm production was exported. It is estimated that the products of one out of every four acres of harvested land in the United States are destined for foreign markets. Specific crop exports are even more revealing; wheat (65 percent), cotton (21 percent), rice (55 percent), and soybeans (42 percent) vitally depend upon foreign markets. (Most of these products are sold commercially but some of them—particularly wheat—are sent as food aid to developing countries.)

Specialized industries such as civilian aircraft (40 percent) and construction machinery (25 percent) also rely heavily upon foreign markets. Machinery and transportation-equipment sales, which account for about one-third of United States exports, earn dollars in every continent. Sophisticated equipment such as nuclear reactors, electronic computers, and X-ray equipment are included in these exports, as well as simpler household items like electric irons, ranges, and refrigerators. Transportation equipment includes varied items such as passenger cars, trucks, and buses, in addition to aircraft and diesel locomotives. Other manufactured goods sent abroad include a variety of everyday items we see around us in department stores and supermarkets, for example, textiles, hand tools, glassware, stationery equipment, and canned goods.

Even these few figures and facts should indicate that many incomes, jobs, and profits are directly dependent upon sales in foreign markets. (Three-fourths of our exports come from 10 industries with the highest wages in the country!) Indeed, one might also say that the entire economy shares this dependence. The loss of a $33.6 billion market would be felt in the form of a multiplier effect: The receivers of incomes and profits from the sum would have less purchasing power, and, in turn, this decreased purchasing power would affect still others who have come to depend upon them. In point of fact, recessions have started in recent years with a falling off in business of less than one-third of the amount involved in the export market. In terms of employment, it has been estimated by the Bureau of Labor Statistics that each billion dollars in United States merchandise exports accounts for jobs for some 91,000 American workers.

WE NEED IMPORTS

Imports, as we have all been told so often, are vital to many areas of the economy and are important to its growth. But the need for imports can be seen on a more personal level. Our rapid means of communication and transportation would not be possible without the 50 imported raw materials necessary for the functioning of our telephone systems, or the 30 raw materials from abroad that help to power our automobiles. The radio and television industries similarly make demands upon foreign raw materials, to say nothing of our newspapers, which depend almost exclusively on newsprint from Canada, Finland, and other foreign countries.

Even if you are not aware that most of the tin in your food cans and most of the bauxite in your aluminum pots and pans are imported, you are aware of the foreign-grown products you put into them: coffee, tea, cocoa, and spices. Whether or not you like bananas, as a statistic you eat 18 pounds a year, helping to account for the 3½ billion pounds imported annually.

Coffee, natural rubber, natural industrial diamonds, platinum, and nickel are, as any schoolboy knows, strictly products of other countries. Some products do originate here, but not in sufficient quantities to satisfy the enormous demands of our gigantic economy; included in this group of imports are iron ore, chrome, tungsten, manganese, petroleum, cobalt, copper, antimony, and bauxite. Not included in the category of imports necessary for the functioning of our economy, but nevertheless important for raising standards of living, are such items as gourmet foods (which are now found on supermarket shelves), perfumes, cashmere fibers, diamonds, distinctive pottery, glassware, furniture, and rugs. In 1968 the total bill for all imports of merchandise amounted to $33 billion. Impressive as this figure is, its breakdown is even more revealing: For example, the United States purchases more than one-half of the world's output of coffee, tin, and rubber. Obviously, imports play a vital role in our economy and help to make life more pleasant. They bring us essential foods and vital raw materials as well as manufactured goods—listed in the following table—which others can produce more economically than we.

INVESTING ABROAD

Exports and imports are the most visible expressions of international economics. Investments in foreign lands constitute an additional important segment of international economics. Thus the world's greatest trader is also the major world banker and financier. Foreign investments serve as a major source of funds for the developing nations. In developed areas, investments often take the form of branches or new factories for existing American companies.

In the next chapter we will investigate more fully the role of the United States as the major source of loans and grants to developing countries. Here, it may be pointed out, many of these investments help developing economies to the point where they will become better customers, hopefully of our products. No such guarantees can be made, of course, because developing nations, like customers everywhere, will seek the best buys available—and these may be found in markets other than our own. It must be remembered, however, that most of our trade is with *developed* countries. The reason for this is simple: Canada, a developed nation of only 20 million people, is our best customer because its people have high incomes, which make possible high standards of living. In 1966 the goods exported to Canada were valued 7 times higher than those sold to India, a country of 500 million people. The $6.5 billion in exports to Canada, at the top of our export list, also may be compared with the $102 million in American goods sent to Nigeria, a country of 60 million, at the bottom of the export list. How do you sell television sets, refrigerators, and hi-fi equipment where incomes are low and where electricity may be nonexistent? In fact, how do you sell anything to people in some areas where they barely earn enough to eat?

Strategic Imports and United States Industry

Types of Imports	Percentage Imported	Percentage Produced in U.S.
Industrial diamonds	100	0
Natural rubber	100	0
Tin	100	0
Manganese	98	2
Beryllium	96	4
Platinum	95	5
Nickel	92	8
Antimony	90	10
Cobalt	90	10
Bauxite	90	10
Chrome	90	10
Fluorspar	71	29

SOURCE: U.S. Department of State.

Overseas investments help to develop raw materials industries upon which we increasingly rely, such as the iron ore of Venezuela, or the oil of the Near East and Africa. Keeping in mind the dwindling supply of our own natural resources such as iron ore, copper, bauxite, and petroleum, investments in resources development take on added meaning. Properly managed, with an awareness of the varied interests of the developing nation, this type of foreign investment can be helpful both to the investor and to the area whose resources are being developed.

Business investments in developed areas, for example, Canada and Europe, often take the form of branches or factories of existing companies. Thus Smith Corona and Remington Rand have European factories, which produce typewriters for sale abroad. General Motors manufactures automobiles in Canada, Great Britain, and West Germany, and Caterpillar Tractor Company has a factory in Glasgow, Scotland. Such investments serve to increase the profits of the parent companies. They also provide—as do the other investments discussed—important markets for American machinery and parts, and insofar as they increase the incomes of other areas, investments create a greater potential market for more American goods.

Although overseas manufacture is generally not considered a desirable substitute for exports, it is an inevitable adjustment to the growing and changing world economy. As nations become increasingly industrial, foreign competition becomes stronger in nearly all lines of economic endeavor. Overseas manufacture, at the very least, permits a nation to maintain a reasonable volume of exports (machinery and materials) that otherwise might be completely sacrificed. Indeed some 25 percent of our manufactured exports now go to these affiliates and subsidiaries.

WHY NATIONS TRADE

To many, world trade brings visions of great complications and even mystery. Actually, the economic reason for world trade is the same as that for domestic trade: It is best to specialize in what you can do most efficiently (cheaply) and purchase from others what they produce more efficiently. Thus, the principle of *comparative advantage* (as the economist terms it) means that the Midwest finds that by specializing in grain it can trade advantageously with the South, which specializes in tobacco and cotton, and with the Far West, which grows fruit, and so forth. Like people, nations—or sections of the country—trade with each other for the benefit they derive from it. Parties to a trade naturally hope to gain from their exchange. Specialization and the division of labor, as we noted earlier in this book, help to increase productivity. There are more than 30,000 distinct job titles for the varied occupations in the United States. We are literally a nation of specialists, with farmers, grocers, chemists, engineers, teachers, and manufacturers each a specialist–producer by reason of his particular contribution to the economy. At the same time each is a consumer of what the other fellow's specialty produces. This principle of specialization is just as true in the economic affairs of nations as it is in those of individuals.

By specializing in the production of goods that they can make with the greatest efficiency, nations can trade their specialties and buy more of the things they want and need. They also can have many of these items at more reasonable prices than if they had to depend solely upon their own products. A nation buys from others because items either cannot be provided by the country itself, or cannot be provided efficiently.

Certain items can be provided within a country, but not so efficiently as other sources can supply them. Why is this so? We return to the principle of comparative advantage: The productive capacities of countries are quite varied, for nature has not doled out her bounties equally. Differences in natural resources, climate, stage of capital development, and degree of know-how and skills will determine a country's productive capacity in certain specialties. Who has not heard of the Japanese way with transistor radios, the Swiss genius with watches and clocks, the Congo's large uranium deposits, and the favorable Brazilian climate for the production of coffee? Each nation specializes in "doing what comes naturally" in attempting to get the most out of its productive capabilities and thus obtain a comparative advantage over other countries.

This means that a nation will nurture those industries that give it the greatest comparative superiority. Although it may be able to produce many of the same items as other nations, it may not do so as efficiently. Therefore, in order to increase its total production, it concentrates on those industries in which it has a comparative advantage.

Perhaps a simple example will illustrate the principle of comparative advantage. The United States can produce both transistor radios and aircraft, as can Japan. But the United States prefers to concentrate on aircraft, which it can produce more efficiently than Japan because of its superior know-how and tremendous capital investment. Even though it is fully capable of manufacturing transistor radios—and, indeed, there are a number of American firms that do turn them out—the United States finds it profitable to import Japanese transistors. The Japanese are content to import American aircraft and concentrate on transistors, which *they* produce more efficiently. Both countries realize by this interchange that they do not profit by producing everything themselves. They profit by concentrating on producing those goods that best suit their talents and resources.

For the United States, the efficiency of its mass-production methods gives it an advantage in manufacturing tractors, trucks, earth-moving equipment, and oil-field machinery and equipment. Its superiority in agriculture creates distinct advantages in the production of staple crops such as cotton, wheat, and tobacco. On the other hand, the United States prefers to import products that require much manual labor (tea) and those that need little capital investment (transistor radios) as well as strategic raw materials not adequately supplied by domestic sources (iron ore). We also buy from abroad, according to the Department of Commerce, other products that consumers desire for a variety of reasons, such as "price, quality, craftsmanship, prestige, novelty of design or construction, allure of the exotic, or other factors which determine individual preferences."

OBSTACLES TO FOREIGN TRADE

Unlike domestic trade, international trade is subject to the rules and regulations of independent nations, of which there are 120 in the United Nations alone! For one thing, nations do not always jump at the opportunity of practicing the principle of comparative advantage. Too frequently they are found erecting artificial barriers that obstruct the free movement of goods and services among themselves. Then, to further complicate the situation, each country has its own money and its own monetary and banking system. International trade is a far cry from the domestic market of the United States, where 50 states, using a common currency, trade with one another with few hindrances or restrictions. Every sovereign nation exercises some kind of control over the goods crossing its borders—and the manner of payment for those goods.

The question naturally arises, "Why do nations seek to control trade?" The basic reason is "to protect home industries." A nation may seek to protect its own industries against foreign competition by imposing on foreign products import taxes high enough to raise the competitors' price, thus discouraging their entry into the country. Using high tariffs to protect domestic producers from foreign competition is referred to as *protectionism*. By way of example, let us assume that the Triumph Bicycle Company, an American company, can make a profit selling its bicycles at retail for $45, but a foreign manufacturer would be able to make a profit by selling a similar bicycle on the American retail market for $35. If a tariff of $15 is placed on the imported bicycle, then the foreign manufacturer must sell his product for at least $5 above the price of the domestic competitor. As a result, the tariff will succeed in protecting the American manufacturer against foreign competition.

Other methods also are used to limit imports or favor exports. *Dumping* is the practice of selling goods abroad at less than a fair price in order to stifle the foreign production of that particular product. *Quotas* may be set to limit the total value or amount of an imported product. This may be an overall limit, for instance, on all milk-product imports, or it may include specific limits for types of milk products such as cheese, ice cream, or butter. Once the quota has been filled, no more of a particular item may enter the country for the rest of that year. *Import licenses* may be required to import a specific amount or specific value of goods. Exports may be *subsidized,* making special payments to encourage exporters to increase their foreign sales. In recent years the United States has subsidized some of its basic agricultural products. In addition to these actions, there are many other administrative or red-tape regulations, including sanitary rules and laws or practices limiting government purchasing to home products.

Evaluating Tariffs

Of all the arguments that nations give for enforcing protective tariffs on foreign goods, perhaps the most frequently used is that which stresses the need to develop new industries at home, often called "infant industries." Another argument is that certain industries must be protected by tariffs to assure supplies of strategic materials and skilled manpower for national defense. Thus after World War II a tariff was placed on Swiss watch movements. Protectionists claimed that the United States needed watchmakers' skills in case of war. Another justification for tariffs is the need to provide more jobs at home and to protect domestic jobs and wages against the competition of foreign workers who get lower wages.

Economists generally regard tariffs as having an undesirable effect upon living standards throughout the world; however, in order to bring about a smoother readjustment they usually recommend a gradual, rather than a sudden, abolition of tariffs. While it is estimated that tariff reductions would affect only about 25,000 American jobs over a period of several years, they may severely affect certain localities that are heavily dependent upon one industry, such as the glove makers of Gloversville and Johnson, New York. Obviously, there are always special human and economic considerations involved even in general programs of merit.

Economists also point out that it is productivity, as well as wages that influence prices. Productivity, as we observed earlier, results from the use of many factors, in addition to labor. (America's dependence on large amounts of labor-saving machinery, for instance, enables her to sell rice to Asians!) While tariffs may benefit individual industries or sections of a country, consumers in general suffer by having to pay higher prices for products. Other nations, by retaliating and raising *their* tariffs, help to bring about a form of economic warfare, which results in reducing the total amount of goods traded among nations. National efficiency in the proper use of resources is discouraged because the less efficient industries are protected from foreign competition. This serves to keep scarce productive resources tied up when they might better be used in more enterprising industries.

Economists also recognize that nations sometimes choose other goals than that of helping consumers to receive goods at the lowest possible prices. Countries, especially new or developing ones, may choose to stress economic growth at the expense of consumer prices. They may see the building of heavy industry, roads, airfields, and electrical power grids as of more immediate importance than raising the standards of living. Other nations may feel that national defense objectives justify similar priority decisions.

United States Tariff Policy

Until the 1930s the United States maintained a rather high tariff policy. The high-water mark in tariffs was reached in 1930 with the Hawley-Smoot Tariff Act, which resulted in a flood of retaliatory measures. Coming as it did, in the midst of the Great Depression, this measure helped bring about a drop in United States trade of $3 billion in imports and $3½ billion in exports. By 1934 total exports and imports had shrunk from $9½ billion to $3½ billion! In an attempt to break down the rigid barriers to trade, Congress passed in 1934 the Trade Agreement Act. This act gave the President the power to reduce tariffs up to 50 percent in exchange for similar concessions from other nations. Since 1934, as a result of successive renewals and extensions of the original act, our tariffs gradually have been lowered. These lowerings of trade barriers, fortunately, have been matched by other countries. Thus for more than three decades the United States has earned a reputation as a vigorous foe of trade restrictions among nations.

In 1962, the passage of the Trade Expansion Act gave the President even broader authority than the 1934 Act to deal with countries willing to greatly reduce their tariffs. Power was given to decrease any tariff rate by 50 percent, and in some cases 100 percent, of the rate existing on July 1, 1962. Exceptions were made only for essential defense industries and those industries that would suffer severe hardship if tariff barriers were lowered. This new concept, called *adjustment assistance*, provides for a policy of benefits for those industries adversely affected. Federal loans, tax reductions, and technical aid may be provided for industries injured by increased imports brought about by the lowering of tariffs. In addition, displaced workers in such industries are eligible for cash allowances and vocational training during their period of unemployment.

Unlike the original 1934 Act, which was passed during the depth of the depression, the Trade Expansion Act was passed at the peak of prosperity. Both laws, however, have a common purpose: They strongly announce United States commitment to freer trade in an interconnected economic world. "Trade or fade" was the graphic way President Kennedy phrased the need for such action.

The Act of 1962 was based upon the expectation that other countries would match America's willingness to topple trade barriers. Therefore, the United States proposed to the members of the General Agreement on Tariffs and Trade (GATT) that a new round of trade negotiations—known as the Kennedy Round for the late President who initiated the talks—be started to seek further tariff reform.

GATT, created in 1947 in Geneva, represents the principal international organization by which nations engage in tariff bargaining on a *multilateral* (many country) basis. It also attempts to regulate commercial policies by setting forth a code of behavior and a set of rules governing the conduct of trade. By 1968 the original 37 members, including the United States, had increased to 70, representing well over 80 percent of the world's trade area.

After three years of intensive negotiations, GATT succeeded in 1967 in substantially reducing tariff barriers. United States tariff reductions average 35 percent (ranging up to 50 percent) on about 6,000 imported products worth about $8 billion. The effect will be gradual but substantial for both consumers and industry with four annual steps from 1968 to 1972. The Kennedy Round has been called "the most comprehensive assault on barriers to international trade that has ever taken place." These tariff cuts, however, are considered to be of benefit primarily to developed, industrial countries. Developing nations were less pleased, insisting that their earnings must be aided by preferential tariffs on imports from their countries for a limited period, without concessions on their part.

Also displeased were certain sections of American industry, particularly chemical, agriculture, and textiles, which demanded protection. This reaction was to be expected, since the overall objective was to eliminate tariffs that protect domestic industries. As a congressional expert explained: American industry must choose between "getting a bigger economic pie or maintaining some historical division of the economy in which industries retain their dominant or less dominant places." Getting a "bigger economic pie," of course, means participating in the opportunity for increased trade. While the Kennedy Round all but eliminated tariff barriers as an obstacle to trade in a wide variety of manufactured products, its effectiveness can be hurt unless countries continue their efforts to remove the other roadblocks to trade mentioned earlier in this chapter.

REGIONAL TRADE UNITS: EEC AND EFTA

Interestingly enough, the United States, aware of its own history of tariff-free borders among its states, in addition to championing free world trade, also has played an important role in furthering large regional trading units. Most prominent of these is the European Economic Community, (EEC) better known as the Common Market. On January 1, 1958, France, West Germany, Italy, Belgium, the Netherlands, and Luxembourg signed a treaty that was directed toward achieving a complete economic union.

These nations aim to create a *free market* (no tariff barriers) for 180 million people, as well as provide for capital and labor to move freely across their borders. The Common Market also has arranged to have their tariff schedules averaged so that each member will be levying the same duty against the rest of the world. Indeed, in the Kennedy Round negotiations the Common Market, which has become the world's greatest trading unit, provided the strongest opposition to United States policies—especially concerning concessions for agricultural products.

No matter how many new problems the Common Market may create for the United States, this nation remains a strong supporter of the European movement toward economic integration. Economic strength, it is hoped, will enable Western Europe to aid common efforts to resist Communism, to help provide effective assistance to the hungry two-thirds of humanity in the developing nations, and, as a growing and dynamic economy, to provide a greater potential market for American goods. Economic unity, it is also hoped, will diminish the rivalries that led to two world wars.

Similarly, the United States applauded the efforts to another economic union that has as its objective the gradual removal of trade barriers among its members. (It does not provide for common external tariff policies, however.) This group of Western European nations in 1960 formed the European Free Trade Association (EFTA) with Austria, Denmark, Norway, Portugal, Sweden, Switzerland, and the United Kingdom. Now that the Outer Seven, as they are known, have already achieved their free trade area, nearly all are eager to join the Common Market—especially Great Britain. Other free trade experiments include the Latin American Free Trade Area (LAFTA), a grouping of nine countries, and the Central American Common Market, a union of five small nations. Eventually, it is hoped—in spite of many difficulties now present—that these latter two associations will join together for an overall Latin American free market.

Free trade associations, then, serve a useful purpose in their attempts to increase trade by removing tariffs that impede the flow of goods among their members. Nations outside the "club," however, look with some apprehension at the possibility that their own trade may subsequently suffer from an increase in trade discrimination.

OTHER TRADE AREA PROBLEMS

Developing nations are particularly sensitive, because of their unique needs, to possibilities of discrimination. Too frequently they are dependent upon a single primary product (food and raw materials) or a narrow range of commodities. In many cases the demand for these primary products is relatively unaffected by price changes. Hence, when they are overproduced, which frequently happens, prices fall and incomes drop. If the developing countries diversify and industrialize their output, as they are frequently advised, they need additional markets. They need markets for these primary products, which make up 85 percent of their usual exports, and for newly developed industrial products. As we noted earlier—and we shall return to this problem in greater detail in the next chapter—developing nations stress their need for trade policies that will discriminate in their favor. Because of their colonial heritage, developing nations still maintain a certain chip on their shoulders toward the big economic powers. While this position is sometimes more emotional than logical, it is nevertheless strongly and widely held by these nations, complicating already difficult relationships.

Turning to the problem of trade between the United States and the Communist nations of Eastern Europe, including the Soviet Union, we find a condition best described as "stagnant." Although some trade movements of late can be detected with a few of the satellite nations, the overall picture shows that total exports and imports to this entire Communist area constitute less than 1 percent of all American foreign trade. To a great extent this illustrates the fact that difficult political relations between nations—the cold war—have a bad effect upon trade relations. Witness, for example, the complete rift between this country, Communist China, North Korea, Cuba, and East Germany. United States trade policy with Eastern European Communist countries and the Soviet Union is somewhat more relaxed in that we aim to keep the trade doors with them open—except, it should be added, where our strategic materials are concerned.

In any event, improved trade relations, even under a happier political climate, would not promise spectacular results. At present, there are few goods produced in Communist countries that would be in great demand on the American market; at the same time, Communist consumers have limited purchasing power for our goods.

THE BALANCE-OF-PAYMENTS PROBLEM

Up to now we have dealt with various problems of international trade, but we have scarcely hinted at one of the most complicated and difficult of all: international monetary relations. This problem deals with the payments charged and received for the exchange of goods. It is a problem that can be stated very simply: Different countries use different moneys. To make a payment to someone in a country that uses francs, or marks, or pounds, it is necessary to change one national currency into another. When an American importer of British woolens pays his bill, he pays his supplier in pounds unless another type of payment is specified. The British manufacturer needs his own currency to make payments in his own country. Similarly, an American exporter of goods to Britain would expect to receive dollars for his goods. Generally American dollars are sent, or credited, by an American bank to a British bank in terms of pounds. And British pounds are sent, or credited, by a British bank to an American bank in terms of dollars. In this way British banks also can keep American dollars on deposit, which it can sell to British businessmen having need of them. This arrangement, of course, permits American banks to perform a similar service for Americans who desire British pounds.

What an exporter pays in his own money for foreign money is called the *rate of exchange*. For one franc he may pay 18 cents, for one mark 27.3 cents, and for one pound $2.40. Difficulty arises because the use of national currencies for international payments often affects the supply of money in the trading countries. Exchange rates are basically influenced, like other products, by conditions of demand and supply for particular currencies. But most countries, through the International Monetary Fund, try to regulate this market to hold the exchange rates at certain fixed levels, to avoid violent swings in the values of their currencies. Critics of the rigidities of the present fixed-exchange rates argue that they should be scrapped in favor of a more flexible system that permits a currency to fluctuate more than the present 1 percent above or below its decreased value. Ultimately, of course, any international system of payments depends on cooperation.

When *all* money received from and payments made to the rest of the world by the United States are recorded for a certain period of time—usually a year—the record is referred to as the *balance of payments*. It differs from the balance of trade, which deals only with the relationship between a country's merchandise trade imports and exports. The balance of payments includes, in addition to the summary record of merchandise trade, what American tourists spend abroad, the payments for defense goods and services overseas, payments to foreigners for their investments in the United States, private loans and investments to foreign countries, and foreign aid. It includes, of course, what the United States receives from such sources as income from foreign investments, tourists spending in this country, and returns from export sales.

For almost 100 years American exports outweighed imports—in 1967 they did so by only $600 million—and hence our balance of trade has offered no problem. But for nearly every year since World War II, our balance of payments has shown a deficit: More dollars have left the country than have been coming in. In recent years the United States has been in the red for an average of $2 billion yearly.

In a large measure this deficit has been due to heavy spending on the war in Vietnam and to the expense of maintaining armed forces in other countries, with the obligation to pay these countries for goods and services purchased to support those forces. On the average $1 to $4 billion a year are sent overseas in military expenditures, which do not come back in any form of trade. The deficits also arise from gifts to foreigners, both by the United States government and its citizens, in part reflecting some of our foreign aid measures. Mainly, deficits have been building up because we are investing more abroad than foreigners are investing here. Investing abroad follows three basic paths: (1) building or buying a plant; (2) buying stocks and bonds of foreign governments or firms; and (3) buying the short-term (less than a year) loans of foreigners.

United States Balance of Payments—1967
(billions of dollars)

Receipts		Payments	
Exports	$30.5	Imports	$27.0
Travel and transportation	4.3	Travel and transportation	6.2
Other services	1.7	Other services	1.2
Foreign investments in U.S.	3.2	Private investment abroad	5.5
Investment earnings, royalties, fees, etc.	7.4	Payments on foreign investments in U.S.	2.3
Military sales	1.2	U.S. military outlays abroad	4.3
(Aid-financed exports included above—3.2)		U.S. government grants and aid	4.2
Other receipts	.6	Other payments (including errors and omissions)	1.8
Totals	48.9		52.5

SOURCE: Federal Reserve Bank of New York.

When we add up the deficits from all these sources, we discover that they outweigh the credits that we gained from our favorable balance of trade. Since payments exceed receipts, foreigners own large amounts of United States dollars; in fact $33.6 billion. They can keep these dollars in their banks, invest them in American securities, or exchange them for gold. In the past 10 years many foreigners have been changing their dollars for gold, shrinking the stock of gold in the United States by $12 billion, one-half of the total amount. (See chart of balance of payments for 1967.)

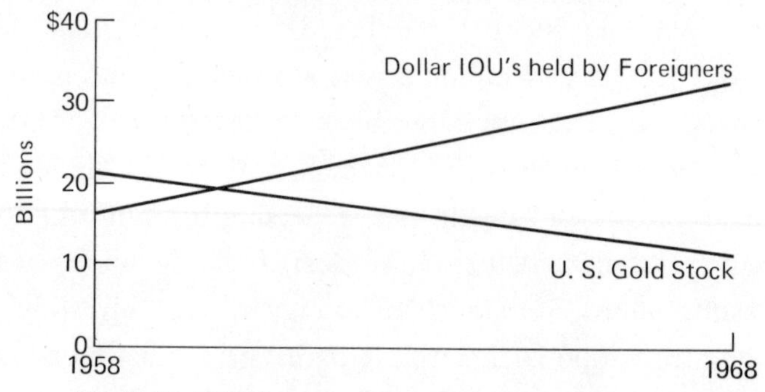

The U. S. deficit has been financed partly with gold and partly with an increase in dollar IOU holdings by foreigners.

Source: Federal Reserve Bank of New York

Fig. 9. U.S. gold stock and foreign dollar claims. (See appendix table 9.)

If the balance of payments deficits continue unchecked (and the problem is a cause for much concern), these deficits might cause further drains on limited gold reserves and thereby weaken the international position of the dollar. In spite of the fact that the real value of the dollar depends on its purchasing power and the strength of the American economy, many nations focus their attention on the payments deficits and the gold losses—and in recent years on the growing inflation in the United States, which, of course, lowers the value of the dollars for all who hold them.

In point of fact, the strength and stability of the United States currency is of vital importance to the free world. Many countries use dollars to back their own currency and to settle business deals among themselves. Undoubtedly this is because we are the only country that guarantees to exchange its currency for gold for government transactions at a fixed rate ($35 an ounce). In effect, this policy fixes the currencies of other countries, in terms of the United States gold exchange rate, with the dollar thus considered as the next best thing to gold. Hence, if others lose confidence in the stability of the dollar, the financial and political status of the United States may suffer. Since many nations hold dollars as reserves to stabilize their own currencies, world trade also may be disrupted. In many respects United States dollars are being used as a kind of international money.

Proposals for Adjusting the Balance of Payments

Major measures proposed to halt the outflow of gold basically involve increasing the balance of trade and reducing the minus signs for the other items in the balance of payments. Improved production methods and greater efficiency may help sell more goods abroad at prices foreigners are willing to pay. Persuading our allies to carry a larger share of the burdens of military preparedness and foreign aid will help reduce expenses. Also, we can make interest rates more attractive to foreigners, so that they hold their funds here rather than in other countries. In addition, as a short-term proposition, banks and industries have been asked voluntarily to trim foreign investments and spending, and tourists have been requested to help reduce the American tourist bill, which removes dollars from this country.

Unfortunately, there is no easy road to improving the difficult balance-of-payments situation. Each of the proposed measures has undesirable or unfavorable results in the light of particular objectives. If we wish to sell more to foreigners, they will want to sell more here; if we restrict imports, they will do the same. Reducing investments abroad may make it more difficult for them to purchase our goods; also, it must be remembered that investments at first are expenses, but later are sources of income. Military spending and foreign aid, in view of today's cold war realities, cannot easily be reduced. Furthermore, the aid programs are tied to domestic spending, and about 85 percent of the total annual economic aid is now spent in the United States; at least one-third of military aid is in the form of goods and services, not currency. Finally, if too sharp a decline is made in United States payments this will mean a slowing down in the flow of dollars, and perhaps too sudden a drop in needed world reserves.

Probably the best solutions are long-run programs, rather than the temporary ones we have discussed. We must maintain a vigorous and growing domestic economy, which will encourage exports, as well as provide opportunities for the investments of foreign funds. We also must seriously negotiate with others for permanent international monetary reform, which will enable countries to build up reserves without today's overdependence on gold or the dollar.

Increasingly, leading authorities believe that the traditional international monetary ties to gold are unreliable and largely unnecessary—as they have proved to be in domestic transactions in the United States. They argue that the community of nations acting jointly should adopt a "monetary system rooted in the full faith and credit" of these nations. Given the strong myths surrounding gold and the persistent power of its symbol, however, it certainly will be some time before the nations abandon the glittering concept of the indispensability of gold.

Fortunately an international agreement signed in early 1968 by nine leading industrial nations (except France) to create a new international money promises, when fully enacted, to ease the strain on world gold reserves. The need for this new money, which has been called "paper gold"—or more properly "Special Drawing Rights in the International Monetary Fund"—stems from the enormous growth in world trade and the shrinking world reserve with which to transact this trade. Briefly, the new system is a checking account plan of managed money, whereby each country is credited with an amount in the International Monetary Fund that is based on its role in the world economy. A nation's balance-of-payments deficits could be made up by drawing from its "bank balance" and paying back at least 30 percent at the end of 5 years. As trade increased, provisions would be made to increase the "paper gold" reserves, just as a nation's money supply grows when increased incomes and business needs demand. Creation of a new international reserve unit is necessary because gold is in short supply (and cannot easily be increased) for the growing volume of trade. And increasing the supply of dollars is not acceptable because of a weakening in confidence in recent years.

Continued international economic integration remains an important challenge for the United States. Our gigantic economy is very much a part of the international economic scene, with its tremendous production, its enormous capacity to consume, its vast funds for ready investment, and the international position of its dollar. For every billion dollars in additional export sales, it is estimated that 91,000 new jobs are created at home. President Johnson had this in mind when he claimed that ". . . an increase in our overseas trade, as all of us are aware, brings great benefits to every single sector of our American life." To bring about these benefits it is obvious that the United States must increasingly cooperate in international attempts to solve the many intricate problems that still beset international economic integration.

CHAPTER 9

DEVELOPING ECONOMIES

Growing Aspirations

In the more than two centuries since the Industrial Revolution originated in Great Britain, a number of countries—including, of course, its former colony, the United States—have overcome the British lead to go on to undreamed-of economic growth. Unfortunately—and this is the challenge—three-quarters of the world's population remain rooted in an underdeveloped past. To underline the challenge even more, the median income in underdeveloped areas is falling, and the explosive growth of population in these sections continues to pull incomes down even lower. While the rich nations get richer, the poor nations get poorer, except in population. Many people in vast areas of Asia, Africa, and Latin America suffer from widespread malnutrition and hunger. Soaring populations threaten to increase famine and the diseases that trail in the wake of the feeble.

President Johnson, in his 1967 State of the Union Message warned ". . . next to the pursuit of world peace, the really greatest challenge to the human family is the race between food supply and the population increase. That race . . . is being lost." Pope Paul VI, in an encyclical "On the Development of Peoples," referred to "those people who are striving to escape from hunger, misery, endemic diseases and ignorance; of those who are looking for a wider share in the benefits of civilization. . . . There is also the scandal of glaring inequalities not merely in the enjoyment of possessions but even more in the exercise of power. . . ."

Essentially the nature of the problem facing the less developed nations is their failure to achieve an adequate rate of self-sustaining growth. True, their annual growth of total output has been rising at the rate of 4.8 percent. Since their populations have been increasing yearly by 2.4 percent, more than half of the growth is needed to maintain their already low level of living. This adds up to a yearly increase in per capita output of only 2.4 percent—less than $3 a person. Two billion people, of the world's population of 3 billion, live in poverty and even subhuman conditions. The ratio of people in the less developed countries who today outnumber those of developed nations two-to-one can be expected by the year 2000 to increase to a ratio of three-to-one. Their annual production of goods and services per capita in 1963 amounted to $160, one-eleventh of that of the richer nations. That fraction, as we indicate, is getting smaller. To take but one specific case: Southeast Asia, an area which happens to have considerable resources, in the past century has increased its share of the world population from 22.3 percent to 32.7 percent, but its share of world income dropped from 11.8 percent to 2.6 percent! On the other hand, the Gross National Product of the high-income countries, now about $1,500 billion, can be expected to grow to $6,000 billion or more by the end of the century.

DEVELOPING NATIONS: THE WORLD'S PROBLEM

The situation of 30 percent of the inhabitants of the globe producing 80 percent of the goods and services has existed for some time. It is only since the end of World War II, however, that world attention has focused on this tremendous problem of uneven economic development. The reason is not hard to find: Most colonial territories joined the ranks of independent nations after the war. Indeed, the new nations of Asia and Africa emerged so quickly that soon they more than doubled the original membership of the United Nations. Economic growth for better living standards—the revolution of rising expectations—rapidly became the rallying cry for the emerging nations. The United Nations became the forum for their historic grievances against their former owners and for their complaints of being neglected, and even abused, by the developing nations. While particular charges might be rebutted, the pleas for assistance widely broadcast by modern communications did not go unheeded. In recent years substantial contributions have been made by the "haves" to the "have nots" in the form of capital funds and know-how.

Translating the $160 yearly income of a person in a less developed nation in terms that are meaningful to an American is extremely difficult. Isolating your annual bills for such diverse items as milk, desserts, laundry and dry cleaning, or entertainment will quickly indicate how far this sum would carry you in our type of economy. American soldiers on rest trips to Asian cities from the war in Vietnam spent on an average $300, bringing the contrast in living standards to the immediate attention of the people of developing nations. Even allowing for their fewer needs (and with no Ford in their future or no pause that refreshes), the people in underdeveloped nations simply cannot obtain on annual incomes of

$160 (and less) the food, shelter, clothing, education, and medical care to meet acceptable minimum standards.

Too frequently the basic problem is "the mathematics of global hunger"—the race between population increase and the food supply. International organizations and governments, including that of the United States, are increasingly concerned over the developing imbalance of population. Numerous efforts are being made to improve this situation including birth control information and the dissemination of birth control devices.

True, statistics on famine and deficient diets are far from complete, and experts continue to argue as to definitions of an "adequate diet." But it is clear from substantial evidence that the undernourished or malnourished can be numbered in the hundreds of millions. Under these conditions, human beings cannot function at their maximum capacity. They are ready victims of disease and ill health; their lack of energy makes them inadequately fit for the drive necessary for sustained economic growth. And because they have low productivity they cannot get out of the cycle that condems them to live on undernourished budgets.

NEEDED: A BIG PUSH

Benjamin Higgins, a consulting economist on many developing projects abroad, compared a stagnant economy to a stalled car: "Leaning on it with gradually increased pressure will not get it started. It needs a 'big push'—a certain minimum level of investment in physical and human resources is required to raise per capita income to the level of self-sustained growth." Hunger and poor diets are obviously among the first obstacles that the "big push" must overcome in the underdeveloped areas. Unfortunately, physical incapacity is but a visible symptom of the biggest obstacle: an undernourished economy.

Curiously enough, while their economies are basically agricultural, the developing nations since 1945 have become increasingly dependent on imported food supplies. Rapid population growth and somewhat better diets have eaten into their recent improvements in output. Thanks to modern methods of fighting disease and of disease prevention, death rates have dropped significantly, although life expectancy is between 40 and 50 years as compared with over 65 for developed areas. Birth rates are now running twice as high in the developing nations as in developed ones. From 1940 to 1965 the less developed nations increased by 54 percent (790 million) to a total of 2.3 billion. During this same period the more developed areas grew by 26 percent. If the population growth rate continues at its 1965 level, the less developed nations will double their numbers by 1980. By the year 2000 Brazil's population will equal that of the United States or the Soviet Union, while the Philippines will have a population larger than that of any country in Western Europe.

Housing and urbanization, already critical problems in developing areas, promise to become acute in the coming decades. Population growth will make it necessary in the next 20 years to double existing housing, sanitation, educational, power and other facilities. It is estimated that within a decade Asia, Africa, and Latin America will have 360 cities with populations of at least a half-million. An Economic and Social Council report (1969) complained of "exploding cities in unexploding economies". It bemoaned the fact that throughout the developing world, the city is faring badly. Many cities, it pointed out, are racing toward populations of a million, while fewer than 5 percent of their inhabitants are employed in industries.

Family-planning programs have been supported by the United States and other nations as a means of reducing the rate of population increase. Thus far these programs have been too limited and are too recent in origin to have had much effect on long-range trends. For food output (particularly grains) to meet the growing population levels, there would have to be an average annual increase of more than 3 percent from 1960 to 1980. Since unusual methods of production and unusual foods are still very much in the experimental stage, this increase will have to come from obtaining higher yields per acre. By way of illustrating this problem it might be mentioned that India has increased its grain output per acre about 6 percent during the past 50 years while the United States has increased its output 95 percent per acre.

Mr. John J. Haggerty, an agricultural geographer, is quoted in the *Morgan Guarantee Survey* (February 1967) as saying: "The truth of the matter is that almost all of the earth's readily cultivable land is already in agriculture, and any further gains in this respect will be very hard to come by, often with fantastic requirements for new research, for technical and engineering skills, and for enormous capital outlay." ("Miracle" wheat, corn, and rice, with their tremendous yields, offer a hope of relief from this dismal situation, however.)

Nevertheless, increased productivity in agriculture is a must for developing peoples. Frequently, the top priority is given to industrial growth for prestige reasons, and agriculture's problems are neglected. Actually, for reasons already mentioned, agricultural development may be a key to general economic growth. Increased agricultural output can reduce the need for food imports; a rising farm income can provide a greater market for the country's industrial output.

Commercial agriculture, farming for the market rather than for the family, must be encouraged, as must agricultural training schools. Fertilizer production is needed, together with agricultural equipment and financing. Better transportation networks to get the crops to local and foreign markets are basic, but difficult, requirements. Credit and marketing facilities are essential, but these take time to develop. Literate, trained farm laborers must be educated to operate farm machinery and to keep accounts. Algeria's 2,300 state farms, which account for two-thirds of the country's farm production, employ 500,000 laborers but only 600 bookkeepers. The administration of a large community in that country does not have a single trained secretary-typist! Incentives for farmers to increase output also are high on the list of basic responsibilities that must be worked out by the less developed countries themselves. Frequently statistics needed for long-range planning in agriculture, as well as for industry, do not exist or are unreliable.

THE PROBLEM OF SAVINGS AND INVESTMENTS

We noted earlier in this book the tremendous need for savings and investment in order to increase productivity. Savings from current production must be channeled into investment for future progress. The simple fact is that the developing nations have low levels of income that prevent adequate savings and capital formation. Too great a proportion of the stock of goods is consumed by the population and hence little is left for future use. Limited savings on a limited income produce limited funds for investments. Undoubtedly funds from abroad are vital for the "big push" required to bring about self-sustained growth. High growth rates are essential if per capita income levels are to be raised, if employment for a growing labor force is to be attained, and if the people's welfare and education are to be improved.

While the Gross National Product of the less developed nations has been rising in recent years, it suffers from the same difficulty as the agricultural sector of the economy: Population increases lower the per capita income. From 30 to 50 percent of the developing countries' GNP is derived from agriculture (as contrasted with less than 15 percent in the developed nations). The effect of growing populations becomes even more obvious when we consider that the proportion of the labor force in the United States engaged in farming is 5 percent, while the average in the less developed areas is 56 percent. Production does not meet consumers' needs in food, but food takes 70 percent of the budget as compared with 20 percent in the United States.

Exports, tied as they are in the developing nations to one or two basic raw materials or agricultural products, present another problem. With all their eggs in one basket (27 of these nations receive 50 percent or more of their foreign exchange from one commodity), their exports are susceptible to wider swings in prices than manufactured goods. With few other specialties to fall back upon, they are vulnerable to loss of business because of synthetics or substitute products. Malaysia's rubber has been hurt by synthetic rubber. Venezuela's reliance on oil (91 percent) is continually upset by new discoveries of competing oil in other parts of the world. East Africa's stronger coffee blends meet the growing demand for instant coffee, and Brazil's warehouses bulge with sacks of unsold beans.

Lacking industry, the developing countries cannot produce the specialized items wanted in developed countries. With a scarcity of technical skills needed for producing innovations, they find it difficult to concentrate on the most highly valued exports that demand these skills. Although exports have expanded in the 1960s, the rate of growth has been less than that of total trade. Therefore the developing nations' relative share of world trade has declined from 27 percent in 1953 to 20 percent in 1967.

Unfortunately, there are additional reasons why underdeveloped nations find it difficult to make the "Great Leap" to a developed economy. We have spoken of illiteracy and the lack of training in the many skills required for an advanced economy. There also is a lack of skilled administrators, managers, and entrepreneurs to plan and guide the economy with know-how along the intricate paths of financing and developing industry. In many areas cultural and social institutions still tie individuals to time-honored ways of doing things, which may interfere with changes demanded by an industrial revolution. Landlords usually resist changes in land tenure in underdeveloped economies and thus often make it difficult for peasants to improve their lot or even to find other types of employment. Some cultures may offer obstacles to women working, to fences and private property, and to the efficiency, discipline, and responsibility demanded of workers by modern industry. Class lines in some cultures are stratified, with landed interests in positions of power, making it difficult for individuals to correct extreme social and economic inequalities. Masses frequently are apathetic. And manual labor and employment for wages are held in low esteem by the upper classes.

Dr. Gunnar Myrdal, in a three-volume study issued in 1968 that required 10 years to complete, concluded that the major need is for changes in attitudes and institutions by the developing peoples themselves. *Asian Drama: An Inquiry into the Poverty of Nations* surveys 11 nations in South Asia—one-fourth of mankind—and concludes that aid from the West, while crucial to destitute people, is at best a marginal factor. Dr. Myrdal foresaw increasing misery and "explosive potentialities" unless basic institutional changes were made. He advocated birth control, land reform to give incentives to those now working the land, and urged an overhaul of an educational system now oriented "for poverty." So great are development difficulties that Dr. Myrdal saw the need for more Gandhis "who would sway the upper classes and who would walk the country roads and inspire the people in their villages."

Political regimes may be unstable or corrupt and discourage native and foreign investors from taking a chance on projects in their country. Dictatorial regimes may be more interested in building military machines than in improving their agricultural and industrial situation. Often "prestige industries" (such as airlines or steel industries) are promoted at the expense of more necessary enterprises. Relatively inexpensive ground water-storage systems are passed over for large and costly dams. Shaky, uneconomic industries frequently receive injections of public funds to keep them going. Honest and competent civil servants are not conspicuously present in great numbers in most developing nations. Under these conditions there is an absence of effective economic leadership and a waste of natural and human resources. The net result, as it has been pointed out by a former president of the World Bank "is likely to be public apathy and cynicism instead of the ferment and enthusiasm needed for economic progress."

Development analysts at Yale's Economic Growth Center, after surveying Latin America, Asia, and Africa, concluded that "any economist who thinks he can sit in the United States today and analyze the problems of growth in the emerging countries on the basis of available statistics is hopelessly naive." On-the-spot research soon reveals the great differences among the developing nations. Political instability or actual disunity may trouble some countries; others may suffer from a shortage of foreign exchange; still others are troubled by inflation; and some may be concerned about the sudden explosion of urban unemployment. One country may have one or several of these problems; a few may have all of them.

Yet in spite of all these difficulties one strong ray of hope remains, aside from the increasing responses of developed nations: The most costly education—the practical experience gained by the trial and error of the new-nation builders—may yet prove the most valuable. After a generation of meeting the persistent problems involved in making their economies grow, private entrepreneurs and government officials in the developing nations are discovering some solutions. And as expert observers have noted, in the words of President Johnson, "Economic and social development is a task not for sprinters, but for long-distance runners."

Certain less developed countries, among them Israel, Malaysia, Taiwan, and some countries of Central America, already have attained self-sustaining growth. Approaching that objective are Pakistan, South Korea, Thailand, and Turkey. According to the 1967 *Economic Report of the President,* "The pace of economic expansion achieved by the less developed countries is encouraging." Skills required for a modern economy are being developed. And some countries are now "capable of using more capital than they can raise domestically or borrow abroad on commercial terms."

FOREIGN AID

Foreign aid, both from the resources of high-income countries and international organizations, is a vital necessity for the developing nations. Yet this aid, which should be increasing, has lagged or even stagnated during a period when the industrial countries reached new heights of prosperity. Although the wealth of the donor countries increased by $250 billion from 1961 to 1966, the total annual aid remained constant at about $6 billion. The goal of 1 percent of a nation's GNP for aid purposes has never been reached by any country, including the United States. Judging by the recent mounting opposition in Congress to the present level of aid payments, the chances are slim indeed that the United States will meet this objective. It seems that popular support for foreign aid has diminished in Western and Communist countries because of lingering doubts about the effectiveness of governmental programs, compelling needs at home, and international payments problems. A minimum estimate states that the developing countries need $4 billion more than they are getting from public funds.

About one-fourth of the funds needed for domestic growth in the developing countries comes from outside their boundaries. Since 1963 the increase has come entirely from private sources for investment. These funds have been mainly concentrated in the extractive industries, particularly oil, but unfortunately, many countries lack these industries. And while investments provide needed foreign exchange and technological know-how for the nations rich in minerals, even they do not fully benefit from this type of investment because investment in technologically advanced, sometimes highly automated, extractive processes does not have the same stimulating effects on general economic activity as does investment in local manufacturing. Many of these direct private investments, especially in oil, have very little effect upon immediate and even indirect employment. In 1964 more than 40 percent of all American direct investments were in the petroleum industries in developing countries. These investments, it is claimed, "develop natural resources and not people." Training is confined to highly specialized tasks for comparatively few natives employed, and the training has little transferability for other industrial jobs.

Unfortunately, the interest and payments on foreign debts constitute a large and rising proportion of foreign aid itself. Indeed, the debt service charges have increased from 13 to 19 percent (1960–1966) of the total aid of developing countries. In the case of India it has amounted to 26 percent, and Turkey's debt service during 1963–1966 was more than half as large as the total foreign aid received.

For the present amount of aid to remain constant, it must rise in order to cover this growing debt service charge. Since 1963 the increases in debt managed to maintain this plateau. Pledges of future aid dropped off in 1965, however, casting a gloomy shadow over prospects for even maintaining present aid levels.

Reporting to the Congress in 1967, President Johnson strongly declared: "The United States will continue to respond constructively to the aspirations of the developing nations. We will give first priority to fighting the evils of hunger, disease, and ignorance in those free world countries which are resolutely committed to helping themselves. There should, however, be increasing efforts to make both the receiving and giving of aid a matter for creative international partnership."

In 1948 the United States started a program for aiding the developing nations. It also urged other mature economies to join in the movement by contributing capital and technical assistance directly or through international organizations. (The aid "club" *has* grown, so that now France, Great Britain, West Germany, Japan, the U.S.S.R., and even China have joined, albeit for diverse reasons.) At this point it might well be asked why the United States pioneered and has continued to advocate economic progress for the underdeveloped countries.

Has Foreign Aid Paid Off?

Undoubtedly, the humanitarian appeal in the United States is a strong one. That the rich should help the poor is a doctrine to which many Americans will subscribe. However, it hardly provides the sole answer to the question of why the United States spent $123 *billion* for foreign assistance from 1946–1966. Another reason often given for foreign aid is the need to develop friends among the developing nations, to keep them away or wean them away from Communism. Rebutting this argument, it can be pointed out that funds do not always make friends, nor does an improved economy necessarily immunize an area from Communism.

Economic motives also are cited; namely that exports from the United States will be encouraged and that it will obtain needed raw materials. Increased purchases from the United States, however, in one area may be at the expense of those in another export area. Lacking incomes, the less developed countries are unable to import in great quantities the products of industrial countries. If, for example, they increase their quota of American electrical equipment in any year, they may do so at the expense of cutting down on agricultural machinery imports. Studies show that in recent years United States trade with the less developed countries has grown far more slowly than its trade with developed lands. We also may breed competition against United States products in world markets by encouraging production along certain lines. There seems little doubt that if the aid funds were spent at home the benefits would offset any improvements in exports or imports of inexpensive raw materials. The economic arguments for foreign aid are, according to one specialist in economic development, not very strong ones.

Nevertheless, these reasons, valid or not, move citizens and legislators to part with tax dollars. Still, these arguments are probably subsidiary to the basic rationale used by most supporters of foreign aid: the need to support and promote political stability in the developing nations. Foreign aid supplied to governments attempting to develop their countries along lines of solid growth for the benefit of all classes of people bolsters those governments. Unstable governments, on the other hand, threaten the peace and security of their own lands, as well as others. To quote our expert again, "As long as there is a reasonably good chance that foreign aid furthers the kind of political environment needed to avoid political and social disintegration, it represents, in the broadest sense, an efficient use of a developed country's resources." Pope Paul VI in the encyclical referred to earlier aptly described this aspect of foreign aid by declaring that the new name for peace is "development."

Foreign aid is generally thought of as a simple umbrella placed over the heads of the developing nations, whereas in reality several different umbrellas are used. The umbrellas basically aim to cover situations involving economic aid and military aid. While the military aid umbrella obviously is held by the government, economic aid is handled by governmental, semi-governmental, international, and even private agencies. Military assistance, it might be pointed out, constituted about one-third ($36 billion) of the total foreign assistance bill for 1946–1966. This is usually delivered in the form of military weapons or in the training of personnel. Where military budgets impose undue hardships upon developing countries, additional economic assistance is given.

Economic aid includes loans, grants, and the Food for Peace program. Loans are granted mainly for providing capital for industries and for developing the *infrastructure* necessary for an economy: the electrical, communications, and transportation networks that power and move modern production. Chief distributor of loans and grants is the Agency for International Development (AID) in the Department of State, which, together with its predecessor agencies, has distributed about one-half ($43 billion) of economic aid since World War II. The Export-Import Bank, an independently managed, highly autonomous governmental agency, accounts for an additional $10 billion, mainly expended for long-term loans. Other aid funds are funneled through the Alliance for Progress, the Inter-American Development Bank, and various international organizations engaged in assisting developing nations, particularly the U.N.'s World Bank and its affiliates, which have in the past 25 years loaned more than $15 billion for specific development projects.

Since 1954 the Department of Agriculture has conducted the Food for Peace program. Agricultural products in surplus supply are sold to foreign importers for their own currencies, while American exporters receive dollars for the value of goods shipped. In turn, some of the foreign currencies are used for investments in the developing country. Provision also is made for the emergency shipment of free food to distressed areas. India, when threatened by famine, has been aided by the Food for Peace program. Africa is rarely without an annual famine of significant proportions, but the false pride of many of its governments has prevented them from requesting needed aid.

We also might allude to the much-publicized and worthy Peace Corps project, which has supplied many developing lands with enterprising Americans eager to help their fellow-man improve his education, farming, hygiene, and industry. Private organizations, such as CARE, work on a direct, nongovernmental basis, as do other relief agencies.

By far the smallest proportion of foreign aid goes to international organizations engaged in helping the developing nations. Some advocates of increased multilateral (international) aid suggest that such procedure would avoid duplication, would better coordinate needed projects, and, since funds would not be tied to one country, would avoid embarrassing political and economic situations. It is usually pointed out, however, that nations which insist upon certain stipulations (such as purchasing in their own markets) would not lightly turn over to international organizations large funds that they could not control.

It also might be mentioned that of late an attempt has been made to have the developing countries cooperate in area projects, such as those involving irrigation and hydroelectric projects. With few exceptions this has not worked out successfully. Many of these countries have not solved the problem of internal union, which is pivotal to a successful economy. Requesting that they cooperate with their neighbors, no matter how worthy the enterprise, is asking for a political maturity which, like their economies, needs much developing.

How realistic is it to expect "returns" on our foreign aid program? Well, as stated earlier, there is an overriding need to dampen the sputterings of unstable regimes to prevent international blowups. Spending a fraction of 1 percent of our annual GNP for this reason alone is a worthy investment. There is sufficient, if not scientific, evidence that the programs, while far from perfect, have nevertheless kept many underdeveloped economies from collapsing. In some cases the results have been positive; witness again the entrance of Israel, Iran, Malaysia, Taiwan, South Korea, and Venezuela into the self-sustaining economic world.

While the specialty of economic development has itself developed in the postwar world, it is not yet able to provide blueprints for nations to follow. Perhaps the most profound conclusion reached by specialists in this area is that the subject is extremely complex. There is no one factor which will provide the answer to increased economic growth. Nor for that matter is there a pattern of growth which can be observed and transmitted. Each country must be carefully studied and evaluated on its own merits for the policies necessary to carry it to proper development. For that matter, it does not follow that a country's prospects can fully be judged by what it has done in the past or is now doing. The problem—admittedly a large order—is to find out the bill of particulars which suits a specific area and try it out.

As developing nations accumulate more capital equipment they are, however, discovering certain basic problems. Perhaps the most important one is that they are coming to the realization that economic growth requires more than adding a few changes to existing structures and institutions. Generally the process is a slow one involving many difficult problems, both obvious and unforeseen, for the technology of high-income countries simply cannot be transferred intact to the underdeveloped nations. Just as Western political institutions are radically modified by non-Western nations that adopt them, so must industrial and social organizations change when they are transported. Economic progress is often unsettling, affecting existing class structures, the position of women and the family, and old traditions and beliefs.

The problem of two-thirds of the world's population seeking economic development has been referred to as "depressing," as "a horror story," and as "the most vital need of our time." Regardless of one's assessment of the situation, its high priority on the list of world problems cannot be denied. Whatever the methods used or the solutions advocated, there can be little doubt that the present pace of external assistance and self-help must be greatly accelerated. Otherwise, we risk having the world further divided into the very visible rich and the very frustrated poor—"an intolerable economic political fission of the world."

CHAPTER 10

OTHER ECONOMIES

How Others Attempt to Solve the Major Economic Problems

As we discovered in Chapter 1, all societies face the identical challenge of the basic economic problem: They must organize social systems in order to choose what to produce, how to produce, and for whom to produce. Given today's rapid spread of knowledge of how well other societies are economizing, there is a heightened interest, and even an excitement, among the people of the world in the vital dramas of production and distribution with which their lives are so intertwined.

We have just seen how the developing nations have become aware that they must accept the challenge to enter the economizing world of the twentieth century. Painfully they grope among diverse examples for economic systems that will suit their own unique needs. Across ideological and military barriers the capitalist and Communist nations confront one another, assessing each other's economic strengths and weaknesses, for economic strength is the key to military strength in the modern world.

There is also a certain growing academic interest in observing what the other fellow is doing in his economy. A knowledge of another economy, it may be added, can serve to reinforce one's understanding of one's own economy. A study of comparative economic systems, if properly conducted, may conceivably remove some of the emotional content from most conversations on the subject. Does not the average person generally proceed on the assumption that there is only one natural or normal way of running an economy? His own, of course. Yet how little he knows about the basic similarities and the real differences among diverse economies: differences which go beyond slogans and name-calling and chauvinism. Here, then, is an area of conflict, with highly emotional value judgments. The economist, with his more objective approach, can perhaps supply us with an analysis, which while lowering the emotional content should considerably raise the level of understanding.

At the outset, let it be firmly stated that in no respect are there any pure economic systems operating today. Nor, for that matter, were there any yesterday. Economies in their operations are generally conducted by individuals too practical to follow theories blindly; be they Adam Smith's for capitalism or Karl Marx's for socialism or communism. Economies, in their realistic dealings up and down the byways of everyday commerce, are engines of change, sometimes unrecognizable to succeeding generations. Thus, while the economy of the United States is overwhelmingly one that pursues private enterprise, it nevertheless is mixed in the sense that government enters considerably into the workings of the market system. On the other hand, while Communism, as practiced in the Soviet Union, may be lopsidedly in favor of government enterprise, private business, although not encouraged, flourishes in certain sectors of agriculture, trades, and services. So, it, too, has mixed qualities, albeit in different proportions.

Unlike Pharaoh's slave economy, or the tradition-bound manorial system of medieval times, all modern economies are dynamic. Industrial economies today must use large amounts of capital equipment and rely on extremely complicated methods of planning and production. They must be highly specialized in their output, their labor, and their management; hence they also must be more interdependent within their own economic sphere and with the rest of the world. Since economic systems keep changing continually, and since practices within a particular system vary greatly, it is often difficult to list their policies in broad generalizations. Still, it is possible to state some differences in the way capitalism, socialism, and communism approach the basic economic problem of managing their resources in order to obtain the maximum results from the use of these scarce resources.

MARKET ECONOMIES: PRINCIPLES

Capitalism, which we have throughout this book referred to as the private enterprise or market system, should at this point be familiar to our readers. We pause here, then, for but a brief review of its underlying principles.

As practiced in the United States, these principles of capitalism are based on the private ownership of productive resources. It is "price-directed" by consumer signals, working through the forces of supply and demand. Producers, seeking profits, respond to consumer preferences. Prices indicate changing consumer desires. In order to lower costs and increase profits, producers are motivated to increase efficiency and lower costs. Thus what and how are determined by private producers responding to consumer preference. Prices paid for land, labor, and capital are determined through markets for these factors of production, which reflect their supply and demand.

Again, these are the broad principles, or theories, under which capitalism operates. As we frequently have noted in this book, however, in practice competition does not always freely direct the forces of supply and demand: Prices often are controlled by powerful business or labor interests as well as by government. In recent years this tendency to fix prices has increased, due in no small measure to the changing United States economy with its tremendous growth of big industry and big labor unionism, together with greatly increased government intervention.

MARKET ECONOMIES: PRACTICES

When we turn to the other democratic mixed economies based on the market system, we discover that, if anything, their systems conform even less to the model of capitalism than does the United States. Public ownership (usually of the airlines, railroads, telephone, and other utilities) is generally more widespread. Government intervention for social welfare activities (housing, health, employment, and old age) is also more common. Note that the bar graph relegates the United States to the bottom of the list for social welfare measures proportionate to its GNP. In fact, welfare services in Great Britain are estimated to equal one-fifth of a worker's income. And with the possible exceptions of Australia, Canada, Belgium, West Germany, Japan, and the Netherlands—which resemble us most—the other important democratic mixed economies lean strongly toward government participation in planning and production.

Great Britain, for example, in order to promote full employment and growth, intervenes actively in planning long-range goals for the economy. In part, decisions relating to the use of manpower and materials are determined by the government. There also are controls on the nature of industrial and business investments, as well as regulations on the specific uses of land. Under the leadership of its Labor Party, which came into power after World War II, Great Britain nationalized electric and gas utilities, coal, railroads, some civilian aviation, long-distance trucking, and the Bank of England. However, the Labor Party, although it calls itself socialistic, does not blindly follow this doctrine as far as government owner-

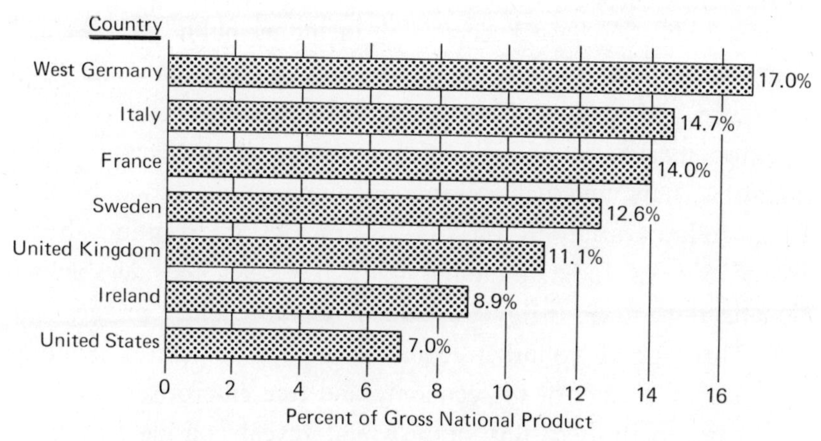

Fig. 10. U.S. social welfare compared to other nations. (See appendix table 8.)

ship is concerned. Its selective attitude toward nationalizing industries can be illustrated by the fact that when the Conservative Party replaced it in 1951, only the steel industry was returned to private ownership. (In 1967, the Labor Party, mainly in the interests of cutting costs, bought 90 percent of Britain's steel-making capacity to operate under government ownership.) While the Conservatives did not pursue government intervention with the same enthusiasm, they did not change the nature of the public thrust into the private economy.

France also has moved firmly in the direction of government planning. There the administration plans a voluntary program for the economy with the aid of business, labor, and agriculture. These cooperatively worked-out plans indicate certain broad lines that it seems desirable for the economy to pursue. There is no compulsion on the part of individual industries to follow the suggested plans.

In France before World War II only the railroad and munitions industries were government owned. Since then, a number of important industries have been added, including public utilities, airlines and airplane manufacturing, insurance companies, the Bank of France, and the huge Renault automobile establishment.

Other market economies, such as those of the Scandanavian countries, Italy, and even developing countries like India and Pakistan, follow variations on the government intervention theme. In the case of India, although there has been considerable nationalization of industries, 90 percent remains under private control. This type of a market economy emphasizes limited planning for the vital sectors of the economy and free enterprise elsewhere.

If space permitted, this study would reveal considerably more variation in the way the democratic mixed economies practice their own versions of the market system. At the same time, it should be obvious that while they all represent a mix of private and governmental decision-making, the economies we have discussed rely primarily on the market system with its private ownership, profit motive, and price policies. And it must also be remembered that government economic policies ultimately are subject to popular opinion in all the democratic mixed economies.

COMMAND ECONOMIES: PRINCIPLES

Strangely enough, the command economies, which are mainly in the Communist nations, also reflect significant differences in the countries where they are practiced.

Just as we outlined the model for the market system as followed by the United States, we might follow a similar procedure in the case of our example of the Soviet mixed, socialist-planned economy.

Central planning authorities, not markets, are pivotal to the command economy of the Soviet Union. GOSPLAN, the State Planning Commission, essentially controls production and distribution.

It determines the central plan, outlining what will be produced. All the major productive resources—the means of production—are owned by the government, with the possible exception of little garden patches. Thus the government is crucial to the all-important matter of allocating resources. It does not wait for "signals" from consumers as to what should be produced. Prices in the Soviet Union are not related to this consumer signal system; instead, price tags are arbitrarily placed on goods in order to accomplish goals determined by those at the top.

If the central authorities favor heavy industries (steel, machine tools, munitions, and aerospace) instead of consumer goods—and this they have done consistently in the past—then prices may be manipulated to discourage the sale of specific consumer items. Keep in mind, of course, the fact that the quantity and quality of such goods are determined in the first place by the central planners.

How the goods will be produced is also determined centrally, with some restricted movement permitted lower officials and production managers to attempt to improve the techniques of production.

For whom (income distribution) is also carefully regulated by the central authorities, who fix wage and salary rates. Since labor may not be privately hired, the only income areas not controlled directly by the government are those in service industries under single ownerships, and in private garden plots. It should be apparent, therefore, that the distribution of income also can be fashioned to aid the goals of the central decision-makers, especially if they should decide to cut back on the production of consumer goods.

As a command economy, the Soviet government, without consulting the consumer, decides what shall be produced, and how investments shall be made and how they shall be financed; it decides how trade shall be conducted and how taxes shall be levied.

COMMAND ECONOMIES: PRACTICES

As in the case of the American market economy, the Soviet centrally directed socialist economy departs from the model. We already have mentioned that a degree of private ownership is permitted. While Communism remains the basic outline, the Soviet economy is undergoing vast and far-reaching changes.

For the first 35 years of its existence, the Soviet Union, primarily agricultural and largely underdeveloped at the time of the 1917 Revolution, turned to increased industrialization with strong emphasis on heavy industry (producer goods) and on the buildup of military capabilities. Since heavy investments were necessary, this was accomplished at the expense of the worker and the peasant, through the regulation of prices, wages, taxes, and production. After Stalin's death, with the achievement of goals to create heavy industry, increasing attention was turned to the neglected areas of agriculture, the consumer, and the worker.

Better incentives and better conditions seem to be in store for Soviet agriculture. Higher wages and prices, bonuses, pensions, more machinery and equipment, greater freedom in private plots, and lower prices at farm stores are promised to the peasants. The government plans to invest more in agriculture in the six years from 1965 to 1971 than it did in the previous twenty. All in all, the harsh, compulsory attitude toward agriculture characteristic of the Stalin days seems to be changing for one more softly inclined toward incentives.

Consumer goods have increased in output, but the general level of quality is still poor. Since there are more goods available, however, consumers have become more selective. Not only more consumer goods, but more varieties of goods have been promised. As the Soviet consumer finds himself in the happy position of being able to make wider choices, the items he turns down will glut the market, increasing distribution and storage costs. This problem of consumer choice and central commands as to what should be produced admits of no simple solution. Changing conditions here, as elsewhere in the Soviet economy, point to necessary changes in their approach to the basic economic problem of allocation.

Reforms benefiting Soviet workers include increased wages, improved governmental labor practices, extended social security coverage, better housing, and a decrease in the level of compulsory government bond purchases. In general, there has been a growing importance attached to the role of income differences as an incentive to production. Soviet leaders no longer refer to the old Communist goal of equality: "From each according to his means; to each according to his needs."

Perhaps the most important Soviet changes in the offing concern planning. As the economy becomes more complex, central planning becomes increasingly more difficult. Consider the 8 million prices for individual goods which, at one time, had to be tagged by the government! In emphasizing quantity, the planners often neglected quality. Local managers, under this overcentralized system, felt no incentive to innovate or to use up-to-date technology. Managers were instructed to meet or to better the output quotas set for their factories; but they were given no authority to obtain supplies. A system of bonuses led to turning out as much as possible with little attention to quality, or to the needs of the market.

A sharp downturn in the Soviet economic growth rate emphasized the need for changes. Accordingly, in 1965 Premier Kosygin announced economic reforms over a three-year period whose objectives were to include: (1) increasing the scientific level of planning, (2) expanding the independence and initiative of firms, and (3) strengthening incentives.

Although the reforms to date have centralized the economy even further, they have also served to give the individual Soviet republics broad powers in planning and related economic activities. Furthermore, managers of firms received increased powers over wages, the number of workers to be employed, and the use of capital allocated to their firms. In effect, the changes help to make the Soviet economy somewhat more responsive to the forces of supply and demand. Many consumers' goods factories can now base their output on consumer demand rather than the central plan. By permitting firms to experiment with a form of the profit motive, the Soviet government hopes to improve efficiency and quality, in addition to the output of its goods. Profits earned by firms may be kept in part for improvements in the business, with the rest going to bonuses for workers and for housing construction.

Central planning, it must be emphasized, still decides the amount and type of products to be produced, and determines the delivery of goods, as well as the wage and salary rates. Other vital decisions that relate to prices, finance, budget, investment, and labor relations are similarly decided. Nevertheless, the reforms will be carefully observed to see how much they contribute to improving the Soviet economy. As one expert viewed the situation, "If the reforms do not go far enough, there will be no further improvement; if they are too far-reaching, however, the whole system of central control may be disrupted." Bureaucratic inertia and opposition, it can well be expected, will long continue to act as a brake on any progress under these reforms. It seems, however, that the reforms do not add up to any definite system that can be described as a radical departure from the established command economy. Nor have the reforms so far revealed the strength to overcome the economic ills which prompted their introduction.

Command economies, although they may have patterned their systems after the Soviet Union, reflect a diversity similar to those we encountered among the democratic mixed economies.

Yugoslavia's brand of Communism exhibits some marked differences from the Soviet Union's. Central planning sets goals and establishes steps for economic development. Output, outside of a few basic industries and for transportation and communication, is determined to a considerable extent by profits, and upon a relatively free movement of supply and demand in the marketplace. The state owns only a small percentage of farms. As a result of this unique mix of socialism and free enterprise, wages are higher and consumer choice wider than they are in most Communist nations. Workers also feel freer to strike (they are not permitted to in the Soviet Union) and peasants raise crops of their own choosing, responding for profit to consumer demands.

Poland does not offer so distinct a contrast in its economy, save for the important fact that its agriculture is completely individually owned. Czechoslovakia recently had been experimenting with increased incentives for workers, the profit motive, and the factors of supply and demand. Plant managers now control hiring policies. Bulgaria, East Germany, and Hungary are more tradition-bound, but of late they, too, have been showing increased interest in forms of decentralized management, profit-seeking, consumer demand, and the encouragement of initiative. Rumania also falls within this category. In addition, it has displayed in recent years a tendency substantially to increase its trade with the West.

By contrast with Communist China, the other Communist nations represent almost liberal economies! China's centralized planning is undoubtedly the most ruthlessly authoritarian of any present economic system. Its five-year plans for industrialization and collectivization of agriculture have been conducted with a degree of brutality that in the Soviet Union seemingly ended with the death of Stalin. High taxes, hard work, and long hours are constant demands of the government, in return for which a meager supply of consumer staples is furnished. Considering its long-range plans for heavy industry for its developing economy and the problem of rapid population growth, it will be many years before Communist China's standard of living climbs above the poverty level.

COMPARING THE ECONOMIES: PRINCIPLES

Despite the many variations we have seen within each type of economic system, some major differences quickly divide the democratic mixed economies from the command economies. On the question of *what* to produce, market economies decide by consumer "votes" to which producers, seeking profits, respond. Under Communism this is decided by a central planning system, which sets prices, quotas, quantity, and quality for a plant manager to follow. *How* and *how much* to produce are determined in a market economy by private enterprisers, but in Communist economies, the government, owning the country's productive resources, determines the priority of goods, their quality and design, and the method of production. In deciding the question of *for whom* shall goods be produced, market economies distribute income in the form of wages, profits, dividends, and rents. These incomes are mainly derived from individual contributions to the economy. Government taxes are used to redistribute income and to transfer various benefits. Spending and saving of income are private concerns. Communist economies also have wage incentives and differentials, but they are determined by the state. Since nearly all the capital goods and natural resources are state owned, personal incomes generally cannot be earned from profits, rents, or interest. Disposable income is further controlled by the government's power to set prices and fix taxes. As a rule, however, more social services are made available by the Communist governments.

Above all, the economic systems are encased in diametrically different political forms. Governments in democratic market economies confine their roles to laying down general rules within which private individuals and businesses operate, and to promoting stable economic growth. Command economies place the *state* first in all matters; not being responsive to the public will, they are less likely to pay attention to the economic needs and desires of their people. Furthermore, there always remains the fear in orthodox societies of a political response when economic reforms prove unacceptable to a leadership distrustful of change. That these fears in command economies are not confined to national borders was headlined in 1968, when Czechoslovakia's general liberalization measures (among which were economic reforms) occasioned frenzied responses from the "old guard" in the Soviet Union, Poland, and East Germany and terminated in occupation.

Such then are the basic differences between the two types of economic systems. We have already stressed the fact that they are similar in having to meet the same basic economic problems. We have noted in passing the variations in each system and the common mix—of private and public enterprise—even though the proportions are quite different. Repeatedly, we observed changes taking place because both economies are specialized in their use of capital equipment and complicated methods of production. While government planning is paramount in Communist nations, it is not unknown in market economies, which, after all, must prepare taxing and spending budgets in advance and must consider certain long-range projects. Money incentives with differentiated wages and salaries are common practices. Social services to supplement incomes in both areas are government financed. And, as recent Communist experiments indicate, the profit motive (keeping in mind the tremendous differences in its extent and use in a market economy) also is to be found in this list of similarities.

COMPARING THE ECONOMIES: PRACTICES

How do the two systems—or at least their main examples, the United States and the Soviet Union—compare in actual performances. What are their economic "batting averages"?

Before attempting a brief survey of economic performances it might be wise to observe a few cautions necessary for this type of comparison. Reliable data for statistical comparisons are not easy to obtain. Both economies operate in different ways and measure their economic activity differently. Command economies frequently treat economic data as security items, or manipulate figures for propaganda purposes. Yet, even where authoritative figures exist, they must be considered in the light of different standards applied by different peoples to different goals and aspirations. Not all peoples value the automobile to the extent that Americans do; few Americans would exchange their material comforts for the simple life that many others prefer.

It is difficult to view the value judgments of others with objectivity. Economics does not eliminate this difficulty, for even measurements like the GNP—which at best are rough estimates—when used as a basis for comparison between two nations are subject to interpretations based upon widely diverging standards. We must first determine how the two areas differ as to their stages of industrialization. Many still consider the Soviet Union a poorly industrialized nation since about one-third of the labor force (as contrasted with 6 percent in the United States) is engaged in farming. Almost 50 percent of the Soviet population is rural based, while only 30 percent lives in America's countryside.

We have, of course, stressed how the two countries use entirely different systems in arriving at economic decisions. We noted, too, the Soviet concentration on simpler types of consumer products. In considering other essential differences that tend to make comparisons unreliable, we must consider varying consumer tastes, which we have already alluded to; the techniques of production, which offer notable contrasts; and the different tax policies and wage structures, which are bound to reflect differences in the prices that serve to measure their GNP.

With these cautions in mind—and they represent only a partial list—about the best we can hope for is a crude comparison of the achievements toward some of the major goals of both economies. Let us draw some rough conclusions, then, on the rates of economic growth, the standards of living, and economic stability.

From 1950 to 1958 Soviet economic growth increased at an annual rate of slightly more than 7 percent. The Soviets succeeded by 1958, thanks to a remarkable annual growth rate of 9.4 percent, in reaching the narrowest margin between the GNP of the two countries. In recent years, as the table below indicates, their average rate has dropped to one slightly over 5 percent, approximately that of the recent United States rate. As a result, given the broader base upon which the United States growth rate operates, the GNP gap has been widening. In 1967 the dollar value of the Soviet Gross National Product was about 55 percent of that of the United States ($426 billion to $785 billion). Dividing this figure by the population for a per capita average, we find that it equaled $1,840 or 47 percent of the average for the United States. Looking to the future, the best available figures indicate that the United States will continue to forge ahead in economic growth on both a total GNP and a per capita basis. Despite some spectacular technological advances in space engineering and war industries, the Soviet Union's GNP is heavily weighted by the contributions of its extractive industries (agriculture, fishing, mining, and forestry). These industries add 31 percent to the Soviet GNP as compared with 4 percent in the United States. However, in the next few decades Soviet technology may draw closer to American achievements, since the Soviet system is avowedly geared to promote industrial development at the expense of consumption, if necessary. In the United States the economy is tipped in the direction of consumption. Hence, as one student of the Soviet economy described the situation, "It should not be surprising if the Soviet system achieves a greater growth rate over the long pull than our own does. It was designed to do so and despite its cruelty and austerity it works."

A closer look at the U.S.S.R.'s growth rate shows it to be rather one-sided in that the investments for heavy industries, defense, and aerospace greatly outweigh those for agriculture and the consumer industries. Savings and investments, prime ingredients in economic growth, are heavier in the Soviet Union, thus reflecting a greater relative burden on its citizens. Resources to produce more consumer goods and to improve the poor performance of its agriculture may result in the slowing of future growth. Further, "the efficiency capabilities of the Soviet economy are inferior to any reasonably developed market economy," a recent major American study on the Soviets concluded. Its efficiency performance has been particularly poor compared with Italy, which is at about the same level of development, but smaller and considerably poorer in natural resources. On the average, Soviet labor is only 50 percent as productive as that of American workers. The United States experience, by contrast, continues to show increasing productivity and impressive growth, while preserving freedoms and the economic advantages of individual initiative. An American can reasonably expect the per capita GNP to double during his lifetime, while the value of the industrial product during this same period will quadruple.

U.S.S.R. and Market Economies: Comparative Growth Rates of Gross National Product for Selected Years, 1956–1967 (percent)

Country	Annual Rates						
	1961	1962	1963	1964	1965	1966	1967[a]
U.S.S.R.	7.0	4.2	2.8	7.9	6.2	7.1	4.3
France	4.4	7.1	4.8	6.0	3.5	4.9	3.8
Germany	5.4	4.2	3.4	6.6	4.6	2.6	−1.0
Italy	7.8	6.2	5.5	2.7	3.4	5.8	5.5
United Kingdom	3.5	1.1	4.4	5.6	2.4	1.6	1.5
Japan	15.3	7.8	6.1	15.6	4.0	9.7	12.5
United States	1.9	6.6	4.0	5.3	5.9	5.8	2.6

	Period Rates (average annual)		
	1956–1961	1962–1966	1962–1967
U.S.S.R.	6.4	5.6	5.4
France	4.9	5.4	4.8
Germany	6.2	4.3	3.2
Italy	6.2	5.1	5.0
United Kingdom	2.9	3.0	3.2
Japan	10.9	8.6	9.5
United States	2.1	5.6	5.1

[a]Preliminary estimates.

SOURCES: Soviet Economic Performance, 1966–1967. Joint Economic Committee, U.S. Congress.

There can be little doubt that the Soviet population's standard of living is markedly better in the 1960s than it was in the 1950s. Soviet consumption per capita has increased from 27 percent of United States consumption per capita to 31 percent during this period. Translating the statistics into goods, the sharpest increases were noted in consumer durables such as radios, television sets, washing machines, and sewing machines. Automobile production did not reflect this increase, although the Italian Fiat automobile company is now building factories in the U.S.S.R., which should add considerably to output. Considering the number of durable goods in per capita use, the Soviets lag far behind the United States. Not only are Soviet consumers limited in the choice of goods presented them, but by their own frequent admission, the quality of the products is poor, as is the service. Statistically, the Soviet consumer only accounts for 47 percent of its GNP, while the American GNP yields 60 percent to this group. It is not uncommon to measure the maturity of an economy by determining the percentage that the service industries contribute to a nation's Gross National Product; in Russia service industries account for 28 percent as compared with 58 percent in the United States (keeping in mind the fact that Soviet government services are included—a not inconsiderable item).

Checking the Soviet per capita after-tax income in 1964, we discover that it was 457 rubles, which, at the official rate of $1.12 per ruble, amounts to $512. For the same year per capita after-tax income in the United States was $2,272. For 1966, net monthly earnings for a Soviet worker with three dependents averaged $106.16 as compared with $453.41 for his U.S. counterpart. Even allowing for the more numerous Soviet free services, such as medical care, economically, the average Soviet consumer is far behind the American citizen. This disparity is quickly revealed in a comparison of how much time and money are needed to buy a typical family's 7-day supply of groceries in various cities.

The "international median" food basket shown below contains one week's supply of staple foodstuffs for a family of two adults and two teen-age children. The contents are qualitatively below the standard U.S. diet and above the average Soviet level.

The Weekly Family Food Basket

Wheat flour	2 kilograms	Margarine	1 kilogram
White bread	3 kilograms	Milk	10 liters
Macaroni	1 kilogram	Cheese (Gouda)	500 grams
Beef	1 kilogram	Eggs	2 dozen
Pork	1 kilogram	Potatoes	5 kilograms
Chicken	1 kilogram	Apples	1 kilogram
Cooked ham	500 grams	Oranges	1 kilogram
Sugar	1 kilogram	Bananas	1 kilogram
Cocoa	100 grams	Tea	100 grams
Butter	500 grams	Coffee (ground)	500 grams

The cost of these provisions, expressed in U.S. dollars and in hours of working time, in April-May 1967, was as follows:

	Cost (dollars)	Working Time (hours)
New York	$18.27	7.3
Moscow	34.60	59.2
London	16.66	13.9
Paris	20.54	32.1
Munich	22.48	21.0

SOURCES: Soviet Economic Performance, 1966–1967. Joint Economic Committee, U.S. Congress.

The Soviets claim that their system is less subject to cycles of recession and prosperity; that it is more stable. In a sense this is true. Central planning, which does not consider consumer demand or profit motives, determines how much shall be invested and how big the supply shall be. Planners can then make arbitrary shifts to keep the economy at full employment. Again, this is done at the expense of productivity and efficiency. A report cited above, in analyzing these factors, concludes that "the over-all level of Soviet technology of 1962 lagged behind the United States by some 25 years."

Although the Soviets maintain stability, they are not so fortunate in avoiding inflation. Since the system emphasizes a high rate of investment in nonconsumer industries, Soviet workers are left with income from these industries with which to purchase the relatively few consumer goods. To hold down inflationary pressure, the government has at times reduced the value of the ruble and virtually canceled the value of government bonds held by its citizens. High turnover taxes, which are similar to our sales taxes, also are used to discourage sales of scarce items.

In spite of the recent reforms, it seems that the Soviet artificially controlled price system is still a major barrier to an efficient economy. To be of real benefit, markets require flexible prices, which truly reflect the influence of demand. This far the Soviets evidently are not willing to go.

Recently, a Soviet economist appealed to his fellow professionals to face the realities of the American market system. He pointed out (a matter of interest to Soviet citizens as well as to Americans) that real wages of American workers had risen substantially since 1945; that United States employers show great willingness to make compromises with labor; and that because of the "Communist challenge" changes have been produced that virtually guarantee that the United States will never have another Great Depression. (The question of whether or not the "Communist challenge" was responsible for economic changes in the United States is in itself an interesting challenge. We can, however, quickly note the welcome opportunity of objectively comparing the economy of others—friend or foe.)

PART FOUR

EPILOGUE

CHAPTER 11

THE CHALLENGE OF ECONOMICS

The Citizen and the Economy

It is axiomatic that an informed citizenry is necessary for proper functioning of a democracy. Most of those who press this claim rarely attempt to spell out the details of this readily acceptable concept. Few, however, would seriously contest the citizen's need for an understanding of economics.

The heart of many of our most vital personal and social problems involves economics. Our economic organization is becoming increasingly complex and important in our lives. We trust that the reader who has come this far in the book concurs with these statements.

Yet economics is a difficult subject with a tendency toward even greater complexity. Indeed, it has been accused of late of developing an abstruseness and a mathematical language that increase the difficulty of communicating its findings to the informed citizen.

Obviously we cannot all learn the craft of the economist any more than we can all attempt to master the knowledge of the physician, the lawyer, or other professionals. But a good reading knowledge of economics is certainly attainable—an introduction to the content, the problems, and the methods of the subject. As Aristotle—an early economist—observed, "Every systematic science, the humblest and noblest alike, seems to admit of two kinds of proficiency, one which may properly be called scientific knowledge of the subject, while the other is a kind of educational acquaintance with it."

Everyone has some acquaintance with economics. Buying, spending, saving, investing, working, and managing all involve the making of daily economic decisions, which not only affect those concerned but in their totality determine the fate of the economy itself. Too often, though, these decisions are based on a fundamental economic illiteracy with a strong admixture of economic fictions and fallacies. Ignorance is strongly related to prejudice; hence "being down on what you are not up on" is as harmful in economics as it is in any other affairs of man.

No physician would expect to have his patient diagnose his own condition. Similarly, the economist does not expect the citizen to diagnose and prescribe a treatment for an ailing economy. The economist does expect the citizen—although he has been delinquent in contributing to his economic literacy—to understand that short-term advantages often lead to long-term troubles. Wage increases, under certain circumstances, may contribute to inflationary conditions, which may actually result in reduced purchasing power of the worker's weekly check. Inflationary times also may call for "stronger doses of taxes instead of an overdose of tight money." It requires no coaxing to enlist public support for tax cuts. But the need for tax increases to prevent inflation—an abstraction to the average citizen—is difficult to "sell" to the public. It is infinitely more difficult, of course, to convince an economically illiterate one.

A modern economy can no more regulate itself without governmental intervention than we can insure the physical health of the community without public medicine. If this is so—and it is difficult to believe otherwise—then it follows that the citizen with a *vote* as well as a dollar must understand the basic principles of economics—the laws, relationships, and forces by which economic systems operate. Only by such an understanding can the priorities, which all economic systems must determine, be properly evaluated. After all, in our democratic society the expert is still responsible to the electorate. Experts may guide but should never dominate. If war is too serious to be left to the military, the economy can hardly be entrusted to the economists.

In the final analysis, the citizen must cooperate in the challenging economic adventure by demonstrating that this country can achieve full employment and personal economic security for all its citizens, together with dynamic economic growth, while maintaining a reasonable degree of price stability and balancing international payments.

Fortunately, there is a wide measure of agreement among citizens in all walks of life about this basic national economic goal. Modern economics can take a good deal of credit for this consensus. For as the *Lloyds Bank Review* of London (July 1965) noted, "the contribution that economics has made, both to public understanding and policy, in the area of employment policy can hardly be overrated. . . . The abolition of large-scale unemployment and of violent swings of economic activity . . . is among the major revolutions of our time." Managing the economic policy to accomplish these goals, as we have noted, is an encounter with narrower social tolerances. Inflation must be curbed, but this may mean that taxes must be raised and the general level of unemployment increased. Who among employed Americans, who now work on the average two-and-a-half hours every eight hour working day to pay their tax bills (federal, state and local), should have their taxes increased, and by how much? How should increased unemployment from inflation curbs be treated, especially if it falls heavily among the minority groups?

These questions, we are reminded by J. M. Keynes, one of the most influential economists of all times, find no ready answers from the economist. "The theory of economics" he says, "does not furnish a body of settled conclusions immediately applicable to policy. It is a method rather than a doctrine, an apparatus of the mind, a technique of thinking, which helps its possessor to draw correct conclusions." Understanding the principles of analysis, however, is perhaps the best insurance that opinion in pursuit of policy will keep away from the detours of biased arguments, especially those which seek to deny government an important role in stimulating higher levels of employment.

While we have broad agreement on the national goal of employment, we must remember that goals and the means of attaining them change. As a result of these changes, coupled with the economy's own inner dynamics, we can look forward periodically to stages of the "new" American capitalism. We do not necessarily mean the scaling of new unprecedented peaks of power and wealth, although these may well continue to be reached. Nor do we refer to the wonders which industry promises to give us: solid electrolyte fuel cells in our homes, laser locks, three-dimensional television, self-contained chemical toilets, and ultra-high-frequency lighting. These are just a few of the more likely prospects.

What we have in mind refers to a changing social atmosphere which is bound to reflect itself in a re-evaluation of goals and in an economy reflecting a greater social-mindedness. Those who characteristically benefit least from the rewards of modern industrial society, the racial and economic minorities, no longer classify themselves with the unrepresented public. Increasingly, their more sophisticated voices are being heard in all varieties of effective forums. Claims are made for a greater share of federal revenues, now rising about $15 billion a year (and an astounding $34 billion for fiscal 1968–1969!). Demands are voiced for more jobs—at understandable lower levels of competency—in industry. And charges are leveled against union barriers that have impeded the access of minorities to the ranks of the skilled.

In eight years (1960 to 1968) domestic social programs increased almost tenfold from 45 to 435. Who has not heard of Medicare, Model Cities, the Job Corps, the "war on poverty" and the myriad Great Society programs? No less than $25.6 billion was budgeted for such programs (up from $9.9 billion in 1960). In a nation which is now 70 percent urbanized these problems show no signs of receding. Indeed, the easiest thing to do is to foresee additional programs to alleviate the problems of our cities: federalization of welfare, revenue sharing, and medical insurance, can be cited as a few of the more obvious proposed reforms.

Until recently the entrepreneur was not expected to consider deeply the probable benefits and costs of new industrial developments to society as a whole. In the past the nation's economic and political institutions granted wide latitude to individual initiative and individual decision-making. With the problems of blight, the pollution of air and waterways, waste disposal, and overcrowded highways regularly featured on TV and in Sunday supplements, business has been forced to consider the broader social and environmental consequences of its corporate projects.

A more sophisticated public, with a somewhat improved knowledge of economics, seeks more from its economy than just the achievement of wealth. It also asks how we can use this wealth for greater human purposes and the improvement of lives. With political power this public naturally turns to government for the accomplishment of its objectives. Not only does it demand government programs, but it seeks additional fringe benefits from business through government and union intervention. Indeed, so pervasive have the social claims of business become, especially through the urban crisis, that one businessman claimed that the real challenge to today's business "is to combine profit and social responsibility—to do good for society while doing well for the business."

This admonition—"to do good for society while doing well for the business"—promises to be *the* tall order for our economic society in the days to come. Fortunately, the American philosophical, religious, and ethical systems have traditions underscoring private generosity and the fulfillment by private persons of public obligations. After the usual fits and starts, needed public service programs are instituted. In the process of augmenting public services the market system, of course, will find itself increasingly surrounded by a more restrictive atmosphere for private initiative.

While the increased needs of the public are generally grasped, the specific needs and their priorities are more difficult to delineate. With this in mind, the U.S. Department of Health, Education, and Welfare in 1969 issued a pioneer study, *Toward A Social Report*. The introduction stated that the reason for the Report was that there now exists "no comprehensive set of statistics reflecting social progress or retrogression." Nor is there any government procedure for periodic stocktaking of the nation's social health. In short, there is no Social Report such as there is an Economic Report required by statute. Only when we attain the sophistication of the social counterpart of the Economic Report can we judiciously decide which social objectives should have the highest priorities. We can then choose more wisely the most efficient programs for achieving these objectives.

With social service budgets continually rising, the public area of the economy is undoubtedly due for more scientific accounting. Cost-benefit evaluations (PPB—planning, programming, and budgeting systems) will help legislators—and the voting public—gain some sense of the economic value of choices being made, and the implicit costs involved. Basic questions will involve the specific inputs and outputs of a particular program and the economic values therein. At present, for instance, we know little about the kinds of outputs the federal tax structure is producing, and the kinds of resource diversions these outputs entail. In other words, in the public expenditure area we are in great need of information about the real social cost and the real social gains to be expected from each social program.

Are we on the verge of changes in our industrial structure? Individual business probably will devote more time to the use of the engineering approach to problem-solving by diagnosing problems, setting goals, and using technology to solve problems and achieve goals. The trend toward less daily human labor with the machine taking over more tasks will undoubtedly continue. From this will flow more leisure-time activities and greater incomes to sustain this life. Personal services, linked to increased income and leisure activities, will continue to rise. Economic processes do not operate in ways that produce instant results; so we must keep in mind the nature of these trends.

As to the economy itself, important sections of which tend to be dominated by oligopoly, advertising, and administered prices, it is difficult to foresee its future in terms of these areas of monopolistic practice. In spite of an antitrust policy, we have permitted the growth of General Motors, whose GNP is exceeded by only about 11 or 12 countries! We continue to preach the need for a greater diffusion of economic power to prevent concentration in a few hands. But our policies in this matter suffer from an ambivalence of feelings, the fear of bigness, and the benefits of size (up to a point). Nevertheless, our unease toward the sheer size of many of our giant corporations continues. What active forms this unease will take is, in view of the incoherent history of the antitrust movement in the United States, impossible to predict.

Finally, the big question arises, will the United States economy maintain its unprecedented peaks of power and wealth? Will it successfully meet the challenges outlined in this book? Obviously, the answer depends upon the two principles we have stressed in the role of economic development: (1) The effort which society puts into development; and (2) The efficiency with which this effort is applied. Again, will economic success continue to come to the United States? The author's estimate is optimistic. However, there is little that can be offered in the way of substantiation for optimism or pessimism! Managing success successfully is far from the automatic process that many conceive it to be. The intangibles that entered into the original success may or may not be present in the future. Managerial qualities will always vary. Domestic and international atmospheres keep changing, sometimes violently.

With a relatively smooth-running and successful economy now functioning, with increased knowledge available as to how to smooth "the bumps" and avoid "the pitfalls," and with a more sophisticated public to appreciate the advice offered by the basic principles of economics, the road ahead is certainly better charted for continued success than those traveled in the past.

Appendix

Table 1. Farm Population, Employment, and Productivity, 1929–1968

Year	Farm Population		Total Farm Employment in Thousands	Farm Output Per Man-Hour (Index 1957–1959=100)
	Number (thousands)	As per-cent of total population		
1929	30,580	25.1	12,763	28
1939	30,840	23.5	11,338	35
1949	24,194	16.2	9,964	57
1950	23,048	15.2	9,926	61
1951	21,890	14.2	9,546	62
1952	21,748	13.9	9,149	68
1953	19,874	12.5	8,864	71
1954	19,019	11.7	8,651	74
1955	19,078	11.5	8,381	80
1956	18,712	11.1	7,853	86
1957	17,656	10.3	7,600	91
1958	17,128	9.8	7,503	103
1959	16,592	9.4	7,342	106
1960	15,635	8.7	7,057	115
1961	14,803	8.1	6,919	120
1962	14,313	7.7	6,700	127
1963	13,367	7.1	6,518	135
1964	12,954	6.7	6,110	142
1965	12,363	6.4	5,610	155
1966	11,595	5.9	5,214	161
1967	10,817	5.4	4,903	169
1968	10,500	5.2	4,745	176

SOURCES: U.S. Department of Agriculture and Department of Commerce (Bureau of the Census) (abridged).

Table 2. National Income by Type of Income, 1929–1968 (billions of dollars)

Year	Total National Income	Compensation of Employees		Business and Professional Income		Income of Farm Proprietors	Rental Income of Persons	Corporate Profits Before Taxes	Net Interest
		Total	Wages and salaries	Total	Income of unincorporated enterprises				
1929	86.8	51.1	50.4	9.0	8.8	6.2	5.4	10.0	4.7
1939	72.6	48.1	45.9	7.4	7.6	4.4	2.7	7.0	3.5
1949	217.5	141.0	134.5	22.6	22.2	12.7	8.4	28.9	1.9
1950	241.1	154.6	146.8	24.0	25.1	13.5	9.4	42.6	2.0
1951	278.0	180.7	171.1	26.1	26.5	15.8	10.3	43.9	2.3
1952	291.4	195.3	185.1	27.1	26.9	15.0	11.5	38.9	2.6
1953	304.7	209.1	198.3	27.5	27.6	13.0	12.7	40.6	2.8
1954	303.1	208.0	196.5	27.6	27.6	12.4	13.6	38.3	3.6
1955	331.0	224.5	211.3	30.3	30.5	11.4	13.9	48.6	4.1
1956	350.8	243.1	227.8	31.3	31.8	11.4	14.3	48.8	4.6
1957	366.1	256.0	238.7	32.8	33.1	11.3	14.8	47.2	5.6
1958	367.8	257.8	239.9	33.2	33.2	13.4	15.4	41.4	6.8
1959	400.0	279.1	258.2	35.1	35.3	11.4	15.6	52.1	7.1
1960	414.5	294.2	270.8	34.2	34.3	12.0	15.8	49.7	8.4
1961	427.3	302.6	278.1	35.6	35.6	12.8	16.0	50.3	10.0
1962	457.7	323.6	296.1	37.1	37.1	13.0	16.7	55.4	11.6
1963	481.9	341.0	311.1	37.9	37.9	13.1	17.1	59.4	13.8
1964	518.1	365.7	333.7	40.2	40.3	12.1	18.0	66.8	15.8
1965	562.4	393.9	359.1	41.9	42.3	14.8	19.0	76.6	17.9
1966	616.7	435.7	394.6	43.2	43.6	16.1	19.4	83.8	20.2
1967	652.9	468.2	423.4	46.3	46.6	14.4	20.3	81.6	23.3
1968	712.8	513.6	463.5	47.8	48.4	15.1	21.0	92.3	26.3

SOURCE: Economic Report of the President 1969 (abridged).

Table 3. Consumer Price Indexes, by Major Groups, 1950–1968 for City Wage Earners and Clerical Workers (1957–1959 = 100)

Year	All Items	Food	Rent	Apparel and Upkeep	Transportation	Medical Care	Personal Care	Reading and Recreation	Other Goods and Services
1950	83.8	85.8	79.1	90.1	79.0	73.4	78.9	89.3	82.6
1951	90.5	95.4	82.3	98.2	84.0	76.9	86.3	92.0	86.1
1952	92.5	97.1	85.7	97.2	89.6	81.1	87.3	92.4	90.6
1953	93.2	95.6	90.3	96.5	92.1	83.9	88.1	93.3	92.8
1954	93.6	95.4	93.5	96.3	90.8	86.6	88.5	92.4	94.3
1955	93.3	94.0	94.8	95.9	89.7	88.6	90.0	92.1	94.3
1956	94.7	94.7	96.5	97.8	91.3	91.8	93.7	93.4	95.8
1957	98.0	97.8	98.3	99.5	96.5	95.5	97.1	96.9	98.5
1958	100.7	101.9	100.1	99.8	99.7	100.1	100.4	100.8	99.8
1959	101.5	100.3	101.6	100.6	103.8	104.4	102.4	102.4	101.8
1960	103.1	101.4	103.1	102.2	103.8	108.1	104.1	104.9	103.8
1961	104.2	102.6	104.4	103.0	105.0	111.3	104.6	107.2	104.6
1962	105.4	103.6	105.7	103.6	107.2	114.2	106.5	109.6	105.3
1963	106.7	105.1	106.8	104.8	107.8	117.0	107.9	111.5	107.1
1964	108.1	106.4	107.8	105.7	109.3	119.4	109.2	114.1	108.8
1965	109.9	108.8	108.9	106.8	111.1	122.3	109.9	115.2	111.4
1966	113.1	114.2	110.4	109.6	112.7	127.7	112.2	117.1	114.9
1967	116.3	115.2	112.4	114.0	115.9	136.7	115.5	120.1	118.2
1968	120.9	119.2	114.9	119.8	119.6	144.6	120.0	125.5	123.5

SOURCE: Department of Labor, Bureau of Labor Statistics (abridged).

Table 4. Personal Consumption Expenditures, 1929–1968 (billions of dollars)

Year	Total	Durable Goods				Nondurable Goods					Services				
		Total	Automobile	Household equipment	Other	Total	Food	Clothing	Gasoline and oil	Other	Total	Housing	Household operation	Transportation	Other
1929	77.2	9.2	3.2	4.8	1.2	37.7	19.5	9.4	1.8	7.0	30.3	11.5	4.0	2.6	12.2
1939	66.8	6.7	2.2	3.5	1.0	35.1	15.7	7.1	2.2	10.1	25.0	9.1	3.8	2.0	10.1
1949	176.8	24.6	9.9	11.6	3.2	94.5	44.8	19.3	5.0	25.4	57.6	19.3	8.5	5.9	23.9
1950	191.0	30.5	13.1	14.1	3.3	98.1	46.0	19.6	5.4	27.1	62.4	21.3	9.5	6.2	25.4
1951	206.3	29.6	11.6	14.4	3.6	108.8	52.1	21.2	6.1	29.3	67.9	23.9	10.4	6.7	26.9
1952	216.7	29.3	11.1	14.3	3.9	114.0	54.7	21.9	6.8	30.5	73.4	26.5	11.1	7.1	28.7
1953	230.0	33.2	14.2	14.9	4.1	116.8	55.5	22.1	7.7	31.6	79.9	29.3	12.0	7.8	30.8
1954	236.5	32.8	13.6	15.0	4.2	118.3	56.5	22.1	8.2	31.5	85.4	31.7	12.6	7.9	33.2
1955	254.4	39.6	18.4	16.6	4.6	123.3	58.1	23.1	9.0	33.1	91.4	33.7	14.0	8.2	35.5
1956	266.7	38.9	16.4	17.5	5.0	129.3	60.4	24.1	9.8	34.9	98.5	36.0	15.2	8.6	38.6
1957	281.4	40.8	18.3	17.3	5.2	135.6	63.9	24.3	10.6	36.7	105.0	38.5	16.2	9.0	41.3
1958	290.1	37.9	15.4	17.1	5.4	140.2	66.6	24.7	11.0	37.9	112.0	41.1	17.3	9.3	44.3
1959	311.2	44.3	19.5	18.9	5.9	146.6	68.4	26.4	11.6	40.2	120.3	43.7	18.5	10.1	48.0
1960	325.2	45.3	20.1	18.9	6.3	151.3	70.1	27.3	12.3	41.6	128.7	46.3	20.0	10.8	51.6
1961	335.2	44.2	18.4	19.3	6.5	155.9	72.1	27.9	12.4	43.5	135.1	48.7	20.8	10.6	54.9
1962	355.1	49.5	22.0	20.5	6.9	162.6	74.4	29.6	12.9	45.7	143.0	52.0	22.0	11.0	58.0
1963	375.0	53.9	24.3	22.2	7.5	168.6	76.5	30.6	13.5	48.0	152.4	55.4	23.1	11.4	62.5
1964	401.2	59.2	25.8	25.0	8.5	178.7	80.5	33.5	14.0	50.6	163.3	59.3	24.3	11.6	68.1
1965	433.1	66.0	29.9	27.0	9.1	191.2	86.0	36.1	15.1	54.0	175.9	63.6	25.7	12.6	74.0
1966	465.9	70.3	29.8	29.9	10.6	207.5	93.0	40.3	16.2	58.0	188.1	67.1	27.0	13.6	80.4
1967	492.2	76.6	30.4	31.4	10.9	215.8	94.9	42.1	18.1	60.6	203.8	70.9	29.0	15.0	88.9
1968	533.7	82.5	36.5	34.3	11.7	230.2	101.3	45.8	19.8	63.3	221.0	76.2	31.2	16.6	97.0

SOURCE: Economic Report of the President 1969 (abridged).

Table 5. Population by Age Groups: Estimates, 1929–1968 (thousands of persons)

July 1	Total	Age (years)						
		Under 5	5–13	14–19	20–24	25–44	45–64	65 and over
Estimates:								
1929	121,767	11,734	22,131	13,796	10,694	35,862	21,076	6,474
1939	130,880	10,418	20,253	14,748	11,519	39,354	25,823	8,764
1949	149,188	15,607	21,634	13,006	11,700	44,916	30,405	11,921
1950	152,271	16,410	22,424	12,839	11,680	45,673	30,849	12,397
1951	154,878	17,333	22,998	12,727	11,552	46,103	31,362	12,803
1952	157,553	17,312	24,501	12,807	11,350	46,494	31,884	13,203
1953	160,184	17,638	25,701	12,986	11,062	46,786	32,393	13,617
1954	163,026	18,057	26,887	13,230	10,832	47,002	32,941	14,076
1955	165,931	18,566	27,925	13,501	10,714	47,195	33,507	14,527
1956	168,903	19,003	28,929	13,981	10,616	47,380	34,058	14,937
1957	171,984	19,494	29,672	14,795	10,603	47,441	34,591	15,387
1958	174,882	19,887	30,651	15,337	10,756	47,336	35,109	15,805
1959	177,830	20,175	31,767	15,816	10,969	47,192	35,663	16,248
1960	180,684	20,364	32,985	16,217	11,116	47,134	36,208	16,659
1961	183,756	20,657	33,296	17,566	11,408	47,061	36,756	17,013
1962	186,656	20,746	33,943	18,483	11,889	46,969	37,316	17,311
1963	189,417	20,750	34,606	19,075	12,620	46,933	37,868	17,565
1964	192,120	20,670	35,301	19,812	13,154	46,881	38,438	17,863
1965	194,592	20,404	35,889	20,637	13,679	46,807	39,015	18,162
1966	196,920	19,811	36,544	21,582	14,063	46,855	39.601	18,464
1967	199,118	19,191	36,965	21,697	15,197	47,077	40,194	18,796
1968	201,166	18,521	37,239	22,106	15,788	47,614	40,768	19,129

SOURCE: Department of Commerce, Bureau of the Census (abridged).

Table 6. State and Local Government Revenues and Expenditures Selected Fiscal Year 1927–1967 (millions of dollars)

Fiscal Year	General Revenues by Source							General Expenditures by Function				
	Total	Property taxes	Sales and gross receipts taxes	Individual income taxes	Corporation net income taxes	Revenue from Federal Government	All other revenue	Total	Education	Highways	Public welfare	All other
1927	7,271	4,730	470	70	92	116	1,793	7,210	2,235	1,809	151	3,015
1948	17,250	6,126	4,442	543	592	1,861	3,685	17,684	5,379	3,036	2,099	7,170
1955	31,073	10,735	7,643	1,237	744	3,131	7,584	33,724	11,907	6,452	3,168	12,197
1956	34,667	11,749	8,691	1,538	890	3,335	8,465	36,711	13,220	6,953	3,139	13,399
1957	38,164	12,864	9,467	1,754	984	3,843	9,252	40,375	14,134	7,816	3,485	14,940
1958	41,219	14,047	9,829	1,759	1,018	4,865	9,699	44,851	15,919	8,567	3,818	16,547
1959	45,306	14,983	10,437	1,994	1,001	6,377	10,516	48,887	17,283	9,592	4,136	17,876
1960	50,505	16,405	11,849	2,463	1,180	6,954	11,634	51,876	18,719	9,428	4,404	19,324
1961	54,037	18,002	12,463	2,613	1,266	7,131	12,563	56,201	20,574	9,844	4,720	21,063
1962	58,252	19,054	13,494	3,037	1,308	7,871	13,489	60,206	22,216	10,357	5,084	22,549
1963	62,890	20,089	14,456	3,269	1,505	8,722	14,850	64,816	23,776	11,136	5,481	24,423
1962–63	62,269	19,833	14,446	3,267	1,505	8,663	14,555	63,977	23,729	11,150	5,420	23,678
1963–64	68,443	21,241	15,762	3,791	1,695	10,002	15,952	69,302	26,286	11,664	5,766	25,586
1964–65	74,000	22,583	17,118	4,090	1,929	11,029	17,251	74,546	28,563	12,221	6,315	27,447
1965–66	83,036	24,670	19,085	4,760	2,038	13,120	19,363	82,843	33,287	12,770	6,757	30,029
1966–67	91,626	26,280	20,554	5,835	2,227	15,505	21,227	93,770	38,233	13,956	8,249	33,332

SOURCE: Department of Commerce, Bureau of the Census (abridged).

Table 7. Civilian Employment and Unemployment, by Sex and Age, 1947–1968
(thousands of persons 16 years of age and over)

Year	Employment							Unemployment						
	Total	Males			Females			Total	Males			Females		
		Total	16–19 years	20 years and over	Total	16–19 years	20 years and over		Total	16–19 years	20 years and over	Total	16–19 years	20 and years over
1947	57,039	40,994	2,218	38,776	16,045	1,691	14,354	2,311	1,692	270	1,422	619	144	475
1948	58,344	41,726	2,345	39,382	16,618	1,683	14,937	2,276	1,559	255	1,305	717	152	564
1949	57,649	40,926	2,124	38,803	16,723	1,588	15,137	3,637	2,572	352	2,219	1,065	223	841
1950	58,920	41,580	2,186	39,394	17,340	1,517	15,824	3,288	2,239	318	1,922	1,049	195	854
1951	59,962	41,780	2,156	39,626	18,182	1,611	16,570	2,055	1,221	191	1,029	834	145	689
1952	60,254	41,684	2,106	39,578	18,570	1,612	16,958	1,883	1,185	205	980	698	140	559
1953	61,181	42,431	2,135	40,296	18,750	1,584	17,164	1,834	1,202	184	1,019	632	123	510
1954	60,110	41,620	1,985	39,634	18,490	1,490	17,000	3,532	2,344	310	2,035	1,188	191	997
1955	62,171	42,621	2,095	40,526	19,550	1,548	18,002	2,852	1,854	274	1,580	998	176	823
1956	63,802	43,380	2,164	41,216	20,422	1,654	18,767	2,750	1,711	269	1,442	1,039	209	832
1957	64,071	43,357	2,117	41,239	20,714	1,663	19,052	2,859	1,841	299	1,541	1,018	197	821
1958	63,036	42,423	2,012	40,411	20,613	1,570	19,043	4,602	3,098	416	2.681	1,504	262	1,242
1959	64,630	43,466	2,198	41,267	21,164	1,640	19,524	3,740	2,420	398	2,022	1,320	256	1,063
1960	65,778	43,904	2,360	41,543	21,874	1,769	20,105	3,852	2,486	425	2,060	1,366	286	1,080
1961	65,746	43,656	2,314	41,342	22,090	1,793	20,296	4,714	2,997	479	2,518	1,717	349	1,368
1962	66,702	44,177	2,362	41,815	22,525	1,833	20,693	3,911	2,423	407	2,016	1,488	313	1,175
1963	67,762	44,657	2,406	42,251	23,105	1,849	21,257	4,070	2,472	500	1,971	1,598	383	1,216
1964	69,305	45,474	2,587	42,886	23,831	1,929	21,903	3,786	2,205	487	1,718	1,581	386	1,195
1965	71,088	46,340	2,918	43,422	24,748	2,118	22,630	3,366	1,914	479	1,435	1,452	395	1,056
1966	72,895	46,919	3,252	43,667	25,976	2,469	23,507	2,875	1,551	432	1,119	1,324	404	919
1967	74,372	47,479	3,186	44,293	26,893	2,496	24,397	2,975	1,508	448	1,059	1,468	390	1,078
1968	75,920	48,114	3,254	44,859	27,807	2,525	25,281	2,817	1,419	427	993	1,397	412	985

SOURCE: Department of Labor, Bureau of Labor Statistics (abridged).

Table 8. Number of Poor Households and Incidence of Poverty, 1959 and 1966

Characteristics of Head of Household	Poor Households (millions) 1959	1966	Incidence of Poverty (percent) 1959	1966
NONFARM	11.6	10.3	22.5	17.6
White	9.0	7.9	19.6	15.3
Male head	5.0	3.9	13.4	9.4
Under 65 years	3.3	2.4	10.2	6.8
Over 65 years	1.7	1.5	34.0	24.7
Female head	4.0	4.0	45.2	37.7
Under 65 years	2.2	2.0	37.8	30.5
Over 65 years	1.8	2.0	59.3	48.9
Nonwhite	2.6	2.4	48.9	37.5
Male head	1.4	1.2	39.7	26.9
Under 65 years	1.2	.9	36.7	23.3
Over 65 years	.2	.3	64.4	51.4
Female head	1.1	1.2	69.4	60.8
Under 65 years	.9	.9	68.1	58.8
Over 65 years	.2	.2	76.3	69.9
FARM	1.8	.6	40.9	20.8
White	1.3	.5	34.7	16.9
Nonwhite	.4	.2	85.0	69.7

The Poor and their Work Experience, 1965–1966 (millions)

Age of Work Experience of Head of Household	1965 Male Head	1965 Female Head	1966 Male Head	1966 Female Head
Total Poor Households	5.8	5.4	5.6	5.4
Over 65 years	1.7	2.4	1.9	2.4
Under 65 years	4.1	3.0	3.7	3.0
Did not work	.7	1.5	.7	1.4
Ill or disabled	.3	1.3	.3	1.1
Worked at part-time jobs	.5	.5	.6	.6
Worked at full-time jobs	2.8	1.0	2.4	1.0
for 39 wks. or less	.7	.5	.6	.5
for 40–49 wks.	.4	.1	.3	.2
for 50 wks. or more	1.7	.4	1.5	.4

SOURCE: Economic Report of the President 1968.

Table 9. United States Balance of Payments, 1955–1968
(millions of dollars)

Year	Exports of Goods and Services						Imports of Goods and Services				Balance on Goods and Services	Remittances and Pensions
				Income on investments								
	Total	Merchandise	Military sales	Private	Government	Other services	Total	Merchandise	Military expenditures	Other services		
1955	19,804	14,280	200	2,170	274	2,880	17,795	11,527	2,901	3,367	2,009	−597
1956	23,595	17,379	161	2,468	194	3,393	19,628	12,804	2,949	3,875	3,967	−690
1957	26,481	19,390	375	2,612	205	3,899	20,752	13,291	3,216	4,245	5,729	−729
1958	23,067	16,264	300	2,538	307	3,658	20,861	12,952	3,435	4,474	2,206	−745
1959	23,489	16,295	302	2,694	349	3,849	23,342	15,310	3,107	4,925	147	−815
1960	27,325	19,489	355	3,001	349	4,151	23,324	14,732	3,069	5,523	4,001	−697
1961	28,631	19,954	402	3,561	380	4,334	23,122	14,510	2,981	5,631	5,509	−722
1962	30,350	20,604	656	3,948	471	4,671	25,305	16,187	3,083	6,035	5,045	−778
1963	32,426	22,071	657	4,151	498	5,049	26,573	16,992	2,936	6,645	5,853	−891
1964	37,099	25,297	747	4,929	460	5,666	28,637	18,621	2,861	7,155	8,462	−896
1965	39,147	26,244	844	5,376	512	6,171	32,203	21,472	2,921	7,180	6,944	−1,024
1966	43,039	29,168	847	5,650	595	6,779	37,937	25,510	3,694	8,733	5,102	−1,010
1967	45,756	30,468	1,240	6,235	624	7,189	40,989	26,991	4,340	9,658	4,768	−1,276
1968	50,219	33,452	1,431	6,819	835	7,683	47,824	33,020	4,511	10,293	2,395	−1,136

SOURCE: Department of Commerce, Bureau of the Census (abridged).

Selected Bibliography for the Beginner

ALEXANDER, ALBERT. *Economics.* New York: F. Watts, 1963.
A brief introduction to the subject.

———. *Karl Marx: The Father of Modern Socialism.* New York: F. Watts, 1969.
Marx's life and basic ideas for the general reader.

———, EDWARD C. PREHN, and ARNOLD SAMETZ. *The Modern Economy in Action.* New York: Pitman, 1968.

BATCHELDER, ALAN B. *The Economics of Poverty.* New York: Wiley, 1966.
The poor, their problems and their prospects, are analyzed in this volume.

COLEMAN, JOHN, ed. *The Changing American Economy.* New York: Basic Books, 1967.
Articles by leading economists on current problems.

COLM, GERHARD, and THEODORE GEIGER. *The Economy of the American People: Progress, Problems, Prospects.* 3rd ed. Washington, D.C.: National Planning Association, 1967.

A general account of how the American economy operates and its future problems.

COUNCIL OF ECONOMIC ADVISERS. *Economic Report of the President.* Washington, D.C.: U.S. Government Printing Office, January (yearly).

A valuable source of information on the current economic situation, together with a look ahead. Particularly worthy for its many useful charts and tables covering the period since 1929.

DUNLOP, JOHN, ed. *Automation and Technological Change.* Englewood Cliffs, N.J.: Prentice-Hall, 1962.

Technology and its effects as viewed by leading economists.

GAMBS, JOHN S. *Man, Money and Goods.* New York: Columbia, 1962.

Economic theory and problems informally and interestingly presented.

HEILBRONER, ROBERT C. *The Making of Economic Society.* Englewood Cliffs, N.J.: Prentice-Hall, 1962.

An interesting survey of the origins and development of the market.

LEE, MAURICE W. *Toward Economic Stability.* New York: Wiley, 1966.

A critical study of stability policies during the 1950s.

MORRIS, BRUCE R. *Economic Growth and Development.* New York: Pitman, 1967.

How growth and development are promoted.

OXENFELDT, ALFRED R., and V. HOLUBNYCHY. *Economic Systems in Action.* New York: Holt, Reinhart, & Winston, 1965.

An evaluation of the economic systems of the United States, the Soviet Union, and France.

ROBINSON, MARSHALL A., *et al. An Introduction to Economic Reasoning.* Garden City, N.Y.: Doubleday, 1967.

Explains how one can view economic problems and what those problems are.

SCHWARTZ, HARRY. *The Soviet Economy Since Stalin.* Philadelphia: Lippincott, 1965.

A very readable account of the goals, accomplishments, and failures of the changing Soviet economic patterns of the past decade.

SHACKLE, G. L. S. *Economics for Pleasure.* New York: Cambridge, 1962.

As the title indicates, the author treats economic theory with a light touch.

SOULE, GEORGE. *The New Science of Economics—An Introduction.* New York: Viking, 1964.

A popular account of the recent changes in the way economists look at the economy.

STEINBERG, DAVID J. *The U.S.A. in the World Economy.* New York: McGraw-Hill, 1966.

International economics as seen through American participation.

WILCOX, CLAIR, *et al. Economies of the World Today: Their Organization, Development, and Performance.* New York: Harcourt, Brace & World, 1966.

A short treatment of the performance of the economies of the Soviet Union, Communist China, India, Britain, and the United States.

Index

INDEX